Treat Them Mean,
and Keep Them Keen

Treat Them Mean, and Keep Them Keen

Gerry Stergiopoulos

■ SQUARE PEG

Published by Square Peg 2008

2 4 6 8 10 9 7 5 3 1

First published in Great Britain in 2008 by
Square Peg
Random House, 20 Vauxhall Bridge Road,
London SW1V 2SA

www.rbooks.co.uk

Addresses for companies within The Random House Group Limited can be found at:
www.randomhouse.co.uk/offices.htm

The Random House Group Limited Reg. No. 954009

A CIP catalogue record for this book
is available from the British Library

ISBN 9780224086172

The Random House Group Limited supports The Forest Stewardship Council (FSC), the
leading international forest certification organisation. All our titles that are printed on
Greenpeace-approved FSC-certified paper carry the FSC logo. Our paper procurement
policy can be found at www.rbooks.co.uk/environment

Printed and bound in Germany by GGP Media GmbH, Pößneck

Dedicated to all the frogs and princes out there.
Kiss both.
But only return calls to the latter.

'A man is like a stamp.
You need to spit on him a bit to make him stick.'
OLD GREEK PROVERB

Just a bit, mind, girls.
Here's how to spit on him in four easy stages.
GERRY

CONTENTS

PROLOGUE

'Make love?
But no one's done that for hundreds of centuries!'
JANE FONDA AS BARBARELLA

Bit out of practice? Don't worry, I'll get you a man.
GERRY

I've suffered to write this book. I spent four months locked in a studio flat, writing. I put on twelve kilos. If Greenpeace ever saw me on my Greek island, they would throw me back in the Ionian sea immediately. I've got a bookshelf with hundreds of self-help books on it. So now I'm really fat, with a really sad bookshelf. Girls, I hope you appreciate it.

I initially wrote this book to help my two female flatmates Mara and Lucy. They are attractive, educated, well dressed, sexy and with great jobs. They tick all the eligibility boxes, but they were also both single. What, I wondered, were they doing wrong?

As I'm a fabulous gay best friend (and as I was really sick of them moaning about it), I wanted to find the answer to their curious conundrum, so I read every dating theory and guide book from the past twenty years. I road-tested their theories, boiled them down to their best tips and looked for the advice that actually works.

I ordered books on body language, read thousands of press cuttings and ordered in biographies of notorious seductresses. (In fact, looking back, I've spent an absolute *fortune* on Amazon and library searches this year

– those flatmates had better be grateful!). I thought back over the years that I've been a confidant to hundreds of women complaining about their men. And to the men, who were all complaining about their women.

I went out and I asked a straight question to my straight male friends: 'What do you want from a woman?' I talked to single women about their dating experiences and disasters. I asked them: 'What went wrong?'

I trawled through my memory. I dug up a few guilty recollections from my own past about lovers who I have left by the wayside. And I looked back on those few mortal blunders of my own that left me in that horrid little category of being The Dumped One. Actually, some of the things I've done really make me cringe when I think back. I'll tell you about them later, so I can spare you the heartache and embarrassment I experienced before I learnt better.

And now I've written it all down. It's taken me months, but here it is. Here are all the answers. The guide to how to treat them mean and keep them keen. For ever. I've tried the tips myself and they work. I found myself some very cute little guinea pigs with six-packs whilst I was writing this book and road-tested being mean on them. I'm still being mean. They're still being keen. (In fact one has just texted for the third time in a row. I'll answer him in a bit.)

I gave the tips to my flatmates and they worked. They've each got a man at last.

And now I'm telling the tips to you, and they'll work

for you too. You, my fine-feathered single friend, deserve an excellent boyfriend. A lover and a partner in crime. This book will help you experience romance that leads to love and maybe – fingers crossed – to a long and loving relationship. Perhaps it will even lead to marriage, if that's what you want. My hope is that this book will change the way you think about yourself and about men and relationships so that you take control of the dating game and enjoy it.

I'll tell you where to meet 'Mr Gorgeous', how to entrance him and what to do at every stage – from the first-date texting rules to that first kiss. (And to that first moment when you slap the little sucker on the knee, say 'not now' and send him home begging for more.) We'll go right up to the moment when, finally, finally, we go to our gorgeously prepared and flatteringly lit bedrooms and, well, as they put it in Barbarella, 'share our delights'. (Don't worry. I've got the being-bewitching-in-the-bedroom bit covered too. After all, who better to tell you the things men like than a man?)

Read this book rather than listening to your girlfriends. Your girlfriends are great girls. They'll make you feel better, and tell you that it's not your fault you haven't got the man. That's all very pleasant, but it's just not true. It *is* your fault.

I'm afraid all this research I've done has made me realise that the vast majority of single women haven't got a man because they say and do completely the wrong things in front of men. You may all be fabulous women, but when it comes to men, you're all *useless*.

Think of me as a friend who actually dares to speak the bare, shocking truth because he likes you. I will tell you how it is, or at least how I see it. Think of me as your devoted dating tutor who will cajole and persuade, sometimes scold you. But in the end I hope I will have given you a few valuable lessons in how to be irresistible to each and every man you set eyes on. I am giving you the tools, and sufficient straight talking and tough love to boost your success beyond your wildest dreams!

Trust me. To get results you must alter your preconceptions, confront your fears. Don't squirrel this book away on a shelf – read it. Act on it! Pass it on to your other single friends afterwards. After all, it probably takes about as long to read this as you usually spend complaining to your friends when you get dumped.

If nothing else, it'll save you the embarrassment of being caught with a shelf full of self-help books with embarrassing titles like *Humped Me Dumped Me* or *Fifteen Steps to Finding a Husband After Thirty*. (Yes, these books do really exist – I've read them all – and there's a list of the ones I recommend at the back.)

Names of case studies in this book have been changed to protect blossoming relationships, naughty little minxes and blissfully happy marriages, but the stories are one hundred per cent authentic, and my advice is one hundred per cent true. Make it work for you.

INTRODUCTION

Why Should I Treat Him Mean?

'My mother said it was simple to keep a man.
You must be a maid in the living room, a cook in
the kitchen and a whore in the bedroom.'
JERRY HALL

Oh, please! I adore you, Jerry Hall, but no wonder
you're divorced. The successful seductress should not
spend all day making wontons, muffins and soufflés.
She'll end up exhausted, with a bright red face and
looking a mess. To keep a man, you should get out of
the kitchen, get into the bath, and make yourself look
fabulous. Order him a takeaway. If you want my tips
about the bedroom bit, they're on page 166.
GERRY

This is the only dating book that gives it to you straight. It does exactly what it says on the tin. It's a book of tough love and tough lessons. You might be shocked at what I suggest, but I swear it works.

Every woman has the right to bag herself a fantastic guy and to find happiness in a healthy and balanced relationship. But there are rules you must play by and mistakes you cannot make.

I look at the way some women behave when they're dating, and, I'm sorry, but it's an absolute car crash. The rules of successful dating are simple, but I bet you've been breaking them all.

The dating game is an art form. This book tells you how to play it. It gives back-to-basics advice on how to get your man. There are things you must lie about, things you must hide, things you must do. Things that will keep the little sucker on his toes.

In Greece we have a name for a woman who bewitches and tempts men. I won't bother you with Greek spellings now as you've got more important things to learn, but it sounds like 'poniria'. A poniria may not be a great beauty, but she can make men do her will without them realising. She's a successful seductress. She has craftiness, guile. She's in total control of the dating game. She treats her men mean and they love it.

Trust me. This is the only way that works when it comes to getting your man. I know from experience. Treating them mean is the answer. Being mean is about being elusive. Not being taken for granted. Not being too available. Interestingly there is no direct translation in English for the word poniria, other than, perhaps, 'lucky bitch'.

Do what I say in this book and dating will be a lot more fun and a lot more successful. Every woman I've passed these tips on to has tried them, *and they've worked.*

So come on, read the book. Let me teach you how to be that lucky bitch.

Why listen to a gay man?

You might be wondering why you should be taking dating advice from a gay man. This is a perfectly reasonable question.

Going gay for dating advice is hardly new. Since the time of Cleopatra, behind every great woman there has been a charming gay confidant. (Cleopatra was *obviously* briefed by gay men. Demanding donkey-milk baths? Delivering herself to Caeser wrapped in a fabulous Persian carpet? Being overly dramatic with poisonous asps? How camp. Trust me. There's no way she came up with *that* little lot on her own.)

Such women have sarcastically been given the title 'fag hags', but I say why the hell not? Better a fag hag than a lonely old hag. Why not go gay when it comes to life advice? Gay men have always been good at making men fall in love. Always. Even right back in ancient Greece, a lot of Greek gods were gay or bisexual. (According to my research, Apollo seduced Hymen, King Admetus of Thessaly, Amyclas and his son Hyacinthus the king of Sparta, Branchus, Cyparissus, Daphnis, Hylas, Iapis, Orpheus, Paros, Phrobas, Potneius, Troilus, Tymnius, Zacynthus, *and* the ram-god Carneius. Not a bad total – and I have it on excellent authority that he made all of them pay for dinner.)

In my opinion there is absolutely nothing derogatory about the term fag hag, and many bright females I know accept this terminology as a badge of honour. Madonna always has hordes of gay men surrounding her. Kylie entrusted total control of her image to the charismatic stylist William Baker, who has stuck with her for years through happiness and illness. What would Grace be without Will listening to her anxieties, suffering when she suffers and, most importantly, providing her with sometimes unpleasant advice that her girlfriends wouldnever dare to give her? And even dating queen Cilla Black asks for help. You hardly ever see her without Dale Winton.

At the end of the day, who knows women better than women themselves? Their gay friends, of course! Women will open their hearts to me because I'm gay. They tell me all the things that they would never tell their girlfriends. I know a lot about my girlfriends. (Too much, sometimes. Some of the things they've done on the first date are *completely* unacceptable. Little hussies.)

Gay men are unthreatening and impartial when it comes to close friendships with women. We are neither in competition with them for the same men, nor interested in them in a sexual sense. We act as sounding boards off which you can bounce your experiences and ideas and when it comes to advice we have a lot to offer you. We are also usually very open-minded, which makes you feel able to discuss your most intimate and darkest fantasies or experiences with us in a way you wouldn't with another girl, however close you are!

And think about it. I'm also the spy in the enemy camp. Men talk to me too. They tell me things. They ask for my advice. They see I'm in touch with my feminine side, and they ask if I can give any clues about what on earth is going on in the big old unfathomable brains of you, our female friends.

And, finally, you should listen to me because I'm a man. I understand the world of men and male modes of thinking. As a gay man I experience the same gamut of emotions and pitfalls associated with dating men and therefore have a deep understanding of how men think.

I fall in love with men too. I've had my heart broken by men. Though I'm embarrassed to admit it, I've also behaved like a male chauvinist pig in the past and broken hearts, cheated, taken men for granted and dumped them.

So I share your world, but I share the world of the men you seek too. That gives me a great insight into the kinds of things a woman will experience when dating. Gay men are almost like ancient Greek sibyls or fortune tellers: we see both sides of the curtain so we have a more rounded understanding of what's going on. And just like the sibyls, we can look at you lot getting it all wrong and predict when a catastrophe is about to occur.

If nothing else, even if you don't want to take my advice on men, at least being my fag hag will ensure you always look fabulous. (I'll be going through style on page 55.)

Listen to me. Do not pay any attention to those silly girlfriends or women who tell you that playing games gets you nowhere. Ignore the old chestnut that goes, 'When I met my partner I wasn't playing any games, and now he's mine.' It's a well-known fact that those who cannot dance say the music is no good. The type of girls that tell you not to play games are usually the ones that have taken a break from the dating game, just like the Dodo is taking a break from existing. They've usually been attached so long that they have conveniently forgotten all the ruses they used to snare their man. Or they've settled for a man well beneath their standards because they gave up looking for something better and said 'yes' to the first one that came along.

You *are* going for something better. And you *are* going to play games to get him.

A brief history of time to explain why being single isn't entirely your fault

'The course of true love never did run smooth.'
WILLIAM SHAKESPEARE

No, men have been useless for centuries.
GERRY

Maybe you think you're the only girl who's ever struggled to get a man, but the problem of how to get a man and then keep him is as old as the world itself.

Dating has never been easy in any age. A cursory glance through literature of all periods shows that the same problems contemporary women encounter when on the hunt for a date have been encountered throughout time.

Shakespearean women were always falling for the wrong men and lying around sighing tragically about unrequited love. Jane Austen's many heroines had to cope with lusting after all kinds of unsuitable types in breeches, and being branded an old maid if they weren't married by twenty-five. And, if you think you've had a long wait for a man, Sleeping Beauty had to wait a hundred years before her prince finally turned up and gave her a snog.

The most glaring difference today is that the modern girl is all on her own when it comes to finding the right man. In every other century, in every other millennium, girls have had help. Dating and relationships have always been, by and large, arranged and closely monitored processes, with mothers, fathers, aunts, relatives and even matchmakers all sticking their penny's worth in the pot.

Medieval women had their destinies decided from the cradle, so never had to worry about things like speed dating. In nineteenth-century Bath, ladies merely visited an assembly room, where they'd be loaned some false teeth to improve their appearance and then paraded in front of would-be suitors to get hooked up. Right up until 1958 in the UK we presented debutantes at 'coming out' parties. They'd be thrust by their mothers in front of an upper-class cattle market of eligible men and told not to come out until they'd got a husband, and a decent one at that.

If you were lucky you got love and commitment. But at least everyone, even the really ugly ones, got a husband.

But now things have changed. It all changed during

the war. Women ran the country as well as much of the war effort in World War 2. When peace returned, they were reluctant to return to their submissive roles. They burnt their bras, slept with whoever they wanted and announced they were free. Instead of biddable housewives we had independent career women. The choice of boyfriend/husband was no longer down to family approval but became a personal choice. Most importantly, dating and marriage was now for love, not for social or familial acceptance.

All well, good and fabulously independent, but this is also the point where things started to get a bit trickier for you single girls. Instead of having a battalion of autocratic and meddling aunts to sniff out eligible suitors, girls now have to do it all on their own. And you have to do it single-handedly whilst juggling university, family, property, careers, friends, and worrying about bikini-line waxing. It's a lot more complicated these days than just shoving in some false teeth in a spa bath.

But girls, here's the secret. *You may have changed. But the rules have not. And neither have men that much.* We've had thousands of years of social conditioning and we can't just shake it off. You, the modern girl, need to learn a little from history. Those meddling aunts of yesteryear knew the tricks for getting a man. The same rules for catching men have worked for centuries.

Girls, it's time to go back to the basics. Think of yourselves as being like the Bennets in *Pride and Prejudice*. I want you to have a game plan, set down some firm rules and *stick to them*. The competition is fierce and ruthless. You must be too. Learn the tricks and you will get your own Mr Darcy. Whether that little bugger wants it or not.

PART ONE

How to Treat Him Mean Before You've Even Met Him

'Men are from Mars, women are from Venus.'

No we're not. We're both from the same planet and
we both want the same things.

GERRY

What do men want?

First of all, let's try and understand our prey. Men and women actually have a lot in common. Men have been dumped. Men have been hurt. Men have been cheated on by ex-partners. When it comes to love, women are not always the weaker sex. We men can be as needy as you and emotionally demanding to the point of exhaustion.

Here is some good news. Men *are* looking for a partner. We *do* want companionship. And we *do* fall in love passionately just like women.

The bad news is that we do it slowly. It takes us a very long time to fall in love because we've got a different biology from you and a different timetable. And the other big difference is that we only fall in love if we think the whole thing has been our idea, and we've been really clever in making you feel the same way about us.

Let me explain why by taking a short romp inside the male brain. (We're really not that complicated. It won't take long.)

We men are simple creatures. We really haven't changed since caveman times. When it comes to dating behaviour men still have rather primitive hunter instincts. Yes, you may well look around you in a bar or office and see perfectly decent-looking males dressed in designer shirts and pinstripe suits, but in fact these male specimens are no different genetically to their prehistoric ancestors who went out in the morning armed with a club, took on a mammoth, killed it and then proudly dragged it home to the cave. Under those designer suits we're all animals. After all, humans share 97.5 per cent of their DNA with that of a gorilla. (I found that little scientific gem in another book I read, *Why Men Don't Listen and Women Can't Read Maps*.)

Like I said, you must go back to basics to make a man happy. You've got to act like those mammoths he was chasing back in his caveman days. The hunter-gatherer instinct is deeply ingrained in the male – we love the thrill of the chase. Too great a degree of availability doesn't do it for men. After all, those mammoths didn't keep texting the men and popping up in their caves in miniskirts to say 'hi', did they? They had to be chased. Men simply don't want the object of their desire to be offered to them on a plate. They want the challenge of the pursuit and capture of elusive and seemingly 'unwilling' prey, just like the cavemen did.

Here's an example from one man I talked to, who explained where it all went wrong with a girl he was interested in.

Richard, 28

'It was all too effortless. I was used to the hunt. She was so nice and so willing to please from the outset that I thought it was too good to be true. She even brought me lunch in the office one day, which was the beginning of the end. I don't want a woman who looks at me like an adoring puppy, all pleading and dependent, so I finished it a week after that.'

Lunch in the office? Oh dear. Now, ladies, that just wasn't very mammoth-like behaviour was it? Taking him in a packed lunch is bizarre behaviour at the best of times, but *especially* in a new relationship. If you must indulge in this sort of thing then save it until you have at least sixty years of marriage behind you.

Basically, even without the sandwiches incident, Richard's girlfriend would have lost him because she was behaving like a complete clot. She was contravening every rule of dating. She thought she was being lovely, being the perfect, adoring, sandwich-bearing girlfriend. But she wasn't. She was just being a clot.

For Richard, there was no pursuit, no delicious uncertainty that gives a nascent relationship its spice. He should have been wondering where she was, not knowing she was in the kitchen hand-rolling wontons for him. This relationship was in the bag far too quickly. This girl was *far* too available.

Girls, this is a common moan from men. You're too nice. If you act like a doormat, they'll walk all over you and then dump you. Trust me. I've dumped men who've acted like this. The doormat act is so annoying. Remember Susie, the sassy Chelsea lady who was the golden ticket winner of *Big Brother*? She adored her husband but refused to iron a single shirt of his before he put a ring on her finger. He bought her a perfect, flawless, four-carat VVS1.

You should be keeping them guessing, making them daydream about you, and hope that you're going to see them again. Richard's girlfriend gave all her power away and surrendered without a fight, like a lapdog rolling over. If you act like this then you'll lose your man to another woman who knows how to play the game.

So that's what men want. The next thing to realise is that most men are bewildered about what it is that *you* want.

They don't know if they should be a macho, dominant man who is the bread earner for the family but is bit chauvinistic and expects to have his meals cooked and laundry done for him, or a sensitive intellectual type who cares about his girl's emotions and every need. The kind of guy who is able to quote Nietzsche until the cows come home, but who thinks it's okay to be a bit of a drip and jump up on the bed with you screaming at the sight of a spider.

Does twenty-first-century man hold the door open and help you with your coat? Or will he risk being on the receiving end of an angry feminist diatribe about equality? Do you want us to be like Gene Hunt or Gene Kelly? If we read the women's magazines for tips it's no help. The standards are impossible. We men are expected to be able to cook, clean, be in touch with our emotions and not embarrassed to share them, dress fabulously *and* be a regular firecracker in bed. Is it any wonder that men end up ignoring their women and spending evenings watching football and moaning at each other instead? Why spend the night trying to do things we don't understand and looking for a G-spot we cannot find, when we could have a perfectly nice time playing on the Xbox instead? We poor ordinary men have as much trouble squeezing into this twenty-first-century-man blueprint as the ugly sisters had squeezing into Cinderella's glass slipper.

And there's worse news to come. Our poor confused little mammoth hunters also have to battle with a biology that makes them total hussies. Mother Nature has stacked the cards against monogamy in a rather cruel way. She has programmed us men to rush around fertilising as many women as possible, and this prime directive is often hard to override.

Men think *incessantly* about sex! Yes, despite all protestations to the contrary, men think about sex on average once a minute. We might be scared of women, you might confuse us, and we might be exasperated by you, but the male sexual impulse is huge. There is often no legal or moral law that we will not brush aside in order to feed our appetites. Men will resort to extreme measures of guile, inventiveness and deceit in order to satisfy their sexual urges. Quite literally – and I say this from experience – it's as if a switch has been clicked on in your head and you go on the prowl specifically for sex, nostrils flaring, breathing heavily, like a bull on heat! If you don't believe me, just try Googling 'Wayne Rooney and brothel'.

Sex is very powerful. In a classical Greek comedy by Aristophanes, the heroine of the title, Lysistrata, manages to terminate the Peloponnesian war just by making all women refuse to have sex with their men until they behave themselves.

But do not lose heart with all these naughty sex-seeking bullocks! Social conditioning and the ability to think rationally have dampened and channelled this instinct with many men. They *are* capable of monogamy. You just have to make sure you learn how to train them and their horns.

This is all sounding a bit biological and scientific, but it's important. It's why I've got lots of advice coming up later on about why you should wait before you sleep with anyone (See the Three-Month Rule, page 137). To catch your man you must learn to channel your partner's sexual appetite so it focuses entirely on you, and then be a calming influence so that things will result in a happy monogamous relationship. Follow the rules in this book, and the man's bull-like approach to sex can be managed along with everything else.

So what else? Men want a mammoth that's hard to catch, they need clear instructions, they want someone to control their horn, and, oh yes, they want fun too.

Most men can be talked into commitment. They just can't be talked into commitment with the wrong, dull woman. Men want fun in a relationship. They won't want a woman who reads recipe books in bed with her face covered in cold cream and curlers on her head. Just like you don't want to be lumped with a dull man who demands his egg boiled for precisely three minutes and wears an anorak and grey leather shoes.

To sum it up, a woman must work on the basis that all men are slightly inferior. They want three things – good sex, good conversation and an easy life. At first it might seem like they just want good sex, but men eventually soon work out that they want all three. It just takes them a little longer to realise it.

So, girls, that's what we're going to learn. How to keep him on his toes. How to train him. How to make him wait for the bedroom bit, and how to be the most scintillating and interesting female of the species. In short, all you need to do to get your man.

What do you want?

This is the part where I'm a bit mean to you. I'm sorry, but I did promise tough love. You need to be told these things.

What do *you* want? What makes *you* tick? Yes, it seems like a simple question. You're reading this book, so you want a man, no? But think hard. What precisely are your reasons for looking for a male? This is a toughie, and you may need to confront some truths about yourself, but you need to be honest and accept your faults. And you need to learn how to overcome your weaknesses, as you'll never get a man if you go moping about thinking that the world has been mean to you.

Do any of the following sound familiar?

Are you desperate?
Are you twenty and you've never had a decent boyfriend? Or thirty, and you feel like you should be settling down? Are you hounded by the terrible tick-tock of biological clocks, husbands, babies, AGA ovens and the logic of your nagging aunts? You're still single and would really rather not be? I suspect you may have desperate written all over you. It's not an attractive look.

Let's look at another case study.

Claire, 24
'I was still living at home with my parents. I was so desperate to meet someone and move away. Finding a partner became like a personal holy grail. I gave my number to whoever asked for it – I was so just grateful they showed an interest in me ...'

Oh dear! This sort of thing just makes me want to weep and howl and bang my head against the wall. Whilst I feel for poor dear Claire, she also exasperates me. She is under the misguided conception that a boyfriend/partner is a 'saviour' figure. If only this (imaginary at the moment) man would turn up – all her problems would be solved. Every man she meets she throws herself at, and waits for him to save her.

Does Claire's story ring a few bells for you? Listen, all this advice you're hopefully avidly devouring will simply not work if you're only seeking a man as a validation of yourself. I'm afraid that a man cannot 'save' you. Men have often been hurt, been cheated on, been messed up and need 'saving' themselves. Think back to Richard's disastrous girlfriend with the packed lunchbox and the puppy-dog eyes. She quite clearly viewed Richard as her saviour from herself, but Richard wanted to run a mile when he saw her looming with a desperate doggy look on her face. The only thing he wanted to save was himself.

Claire, our case study, needs to realise that it is only through her own self-determination that she will achieve her goals of moving out of her parents' house and getting her life together. Her main challenge is to change her mindset. And no boyfriend, real or otherwise, can do that for her. She needs to take her head out of the sand and sort her life out for herself. Until she confronts the problem head-on she will remain stuck in that rut.

As for feeling 'grateful' for attention, this, again, is

a self-esteem problem. Claire feels grateful because she feels unworthy of attention. Wrong, wrong, wrong, girls! A lot of you feel this way, but I have never, ever met a woman who is undatable and not worthy of a good man. Claire needs to make herself feel empowered. I suggest a women's self-defence class, or a local swimming club, perhaps. Even a few therapy sessions might not be a bad thing. Claire needs to recover her self-esteem and independence. Once she starts realising she's fabulous, men will see it too and start taking notice.

Men can smell desperation like dogs can smell fear. If you're too stressed about the biological clock and babies, you'll never be a catch. Men only want women who are not available. Who are not stressed.

I can teach you how to attract men, and what to say and do to make a man want to date you, but if you lunge at him with panic and gratitude in your eyes, he'll run from you and make you feel even worse.

Don't worry if this all sounds a bit familiar. Get working on your self-esteem and, in the meantime, fake it. (There are tips on how to fake lack of interest on the phone on page 121, and tips on how to play it mean on a date on page 127.) And if people start asking you lots of questions about why you're single, just lie through your teeth. Smile, say yes, you're single, yes, it would be nice to have a man, and that instinctively you'll know when to commit. But then smile again and say you are not desperately looking. (Even if you are.)

Don't worry, we'll have you dating soon. Tell yourself you're fabulous, and don't, for heaven's sake, ever offer to make anyone a packed lunch.

Do you keep dating men who aren't right for you?
Here's another case study. Let's call her Nancy.

Nancy, 34
Nancy had been single for about two years; she was feeling vulnerable and lonely and really wanted a relationship. Her parents made it harder by pestering her at every opportunity to find a partner and produce grandchildren. In those two years she had passed the point where she would demand a quality relationship and was now willing to settle for the first thing that came along. She met Paul, who was infatuated with her. He made all the right noises and Nancy got drawn into a relationship with him even though she didn't particularly fancy him and knew that she was using him as an emotional crutch.

Now, this isn't good. Nancy was going for relationship spam as supposed to a prime sirloin. For Nancy it could be Paul, Carlos, whoever ... she just needed someone, anyone, to fill the gap in her life. But she soon found out that having sex with someone you really don't fancy is overrated and her eye began to wander. In fact, a few weeks into the relationship she was already looking for a way out as she couldn't carry on the charade. They split up, leaving poor infatuated Paul heartbroken, and Nancy feeling even more alone, in despair and permanently guilty about trampling on Paul's emotions.

Oh dear. Nancy contravened two cardinal rules here. Firstly she imagined that there was a man-shaped hole in her life, and secondly, due to this thinking, she lost all perspective and overemphasised and overrepresented her singledom to herself, resulting in an 'any man will do' frame of mind. Nancy should have concentrated on herself and gone to the root of the problem a little more instead of projecting all her ills on to 'lack of a boyfriend'. For Nancy, going out with Paul was like putting a chair over a hole in the carpet rather than painstakingly darning it. Yes, it was a quick fix but it didn't ultimately solve anything!

Are you on the rebound?

Hopefully, after dumping your ex you will have taken a militant view of the whole affair. You will have been singing along loudly to 'I'm going to wash that man right out of my hair'.

Well done! But you're still hurting. In this state you are at your most vulnerable and perhaps most irrational. However many of his personal effects you may have set fire to, I bet you're also missing the sex and the intimacy. Going straight on to another man may ultimately be disastrous. Your mood-swings – from clingy

and emotional to militant feminist – will knobble any relationship super-quick!

My advice in this case would be to put this book down, dry your eyes, call some girlfriends and have a pyjama party with loads of ice cream. (Yes, I give you permission to put your 'My Little Pony' pyjamas on.) Let rip. Letting go is cathartic after an emotional shock, and once you've got it out of your system, you can pick this book up again. (By the way, if you're still eating ice cream in your pyjamas five months after the split, that is just sheer indolence and there is really no excuse. Shame on you, dear!)

Are you recently divorced?

It could feel like there's more pressure on you after a divorce, especially if the clock is ticking and you don't necessarily have the springy elasticity of youth on your side. However, look on the bright side. You have now gained important insider knowledge and have learnt from the mistakes of your first marriage, and so will not be repeating them again in a hurry.

Don't give up on marriage, if that's your dream. Happy endings do exist! For every divorce you see splashed across the tabloids, there are another hundred blissfully happy (or at least functioning) marriages going unreported. But that's because nobody wants to read about those. We only want to read about the ones with blood, gore, multimillion-settlements and Heather Mills throwing water over the rival legal eagles.

Are you too busy for love?

Do you feel like you've bitten off more than you can chew in your life? Taken on too many things at once? Do you run from pillar to post, never having a moment to yourself?

Well, maybe you have a lousy boss who works you far too hard, but there's also a chance that you deliberately make yourself too busy because of deep insecurities which lie just below the surface and which will bubble up if your mind is not constantly occupied by day-to-day minutiae. If this is you, if you're plagued with self-doubt that you're not good enough, perhaps it would be an idea to read the biographies of strong women you admire.

Often these women are no more brilliant or endowed

than you or me, and they, too, have made terrible mistakes and misjudgements, but they were driven by a deep sense of their own worth and uniqueness and therefore of the valuable things they could contribute to the world. Learn to let them be your role models and copy their sense of self-worth. Strong, successful women tend to be those that manage to step out of the insecurities that keep many of us tied down. Take a chance on yourself, give yourself a break and dedicate a little time to finding a love that you deserve.

Of course, if you're genuinely too busy because you've got a lousy boss and he or she works you like a dog, then have a scout around, send out a few CVs, find yourself something with better hours and tell the slave-driving boss where to stick it. There's more to life than work.

Are you a bunny bubbler?

Could this be you? Are you a bunny bubbler who simply can't get over your ex? The symptoms of this poisonous disease are (please answer sincerely and tick if they apply):

- You still daydream about him and your time together.
- You still keep cards he sent you years ago or constantly reread his old text messages on your phone.
- You occasionally find yourself dialling his number when you are drunk or bored.

- You keep frequenting a club/gym/street hoping you'll bump into him. (You even drive past his house sometimes.)
- You idealise your ex's attributes.
- You compare every new man to him.
- You spend time talking about him and the 'good old days' to your friends.

Of course, this doesn't just apply to those who've been dumped. Even if you were the dumper, you can still be a bit of a bunny bubbler and obsessed with the ex. Do you feel guilty because *you* dumped *him*?

Let me explain with another case study.

Lauren, 22
'I couldn't stop thinking about him. I called my girlfriends almost daily to lament. I'm so lucky they didn't dump me as well, as I was behaving like a crazed harridan. I couldn't help feeling that this bad break-up destroyed every possibility to be happy with someone else. I simply couldn't mentally cope with being hurt like that again.'

Okay Lauren. First of all, never, ever feel guilty about banging on about your gloomy depressive feelings to your friends. That's what friends are for – and when the time comes, you will support them through their low points. Always talk to people. Don't just sit there on your own in a spiral of self-pity and depression.

Second, there are ways of erasing your past and making a new start which will make things easier. Trust me – you have to do all this if you ever want to stand a chance of getting a new man.

Let's begin with the easy stuff. Have a look around the house. Are there mementos of that old relationship lying around? Any presents from him that you keep even though you shouldn't? (Stuffed toys are always a waste of good bed space.) Pick them up. Walk to the kitchen, get a bin bag. Put the presents in. Say bye-bye. Now either shove it in the wheelie bin outside or, if you think someone else might like it, take it to a charity shop. (Of course, if he gave you diamonds there's no need to be so hasty. You should sell them instead.)

Next, delete that man's number from your phone. You don't need it. Erase all his text messages and emails. Be sure to scrub out his name from address books while you're at it. If you really have to keep his name in your phone for some reason – like he owes you cash – refile it under N for No! No! No! so every time it flashes up it's a reminder that you shouldn't go there. And don't forget about the Internet either – don't look at his Facebook page. Don't go near his MySpace account. What's the point of torturing yourself by noseying around checking what he's up to all the time?

This may all seem hard, but you'll feel better afterwards. It will put a stop to the constant reminders which lead to negative feelings which boil and fester inside you.

Oh, and talking of festering, don't go out shopping when you're feeling bad. You're bound to head straight for the cake shop and gobble up two bags of iced buns like the elephant at the zoo, or, even worse, decide through the tears that a lime-green leotard is the answer to all your deepest needs. (Green does no favours for complexions in mourning. Even the Green Goddess couldn't carry off the Kermit look.)

And one more thing – I hate this slew of myths flying around about how being someone's 'other half' should be a life goal. This is all very cute, but totally untrue. I've had girlfriends who think that because they are single they must be half-people – lacking, wanting – and will only be completed when someone else comes along. What rubbish! We are all infinitely unique and infinitely whole and infinitely worthy of everything that comes our way.

Learn to enjoy your single life. Yes, I know you'll feel bad about it sometimes. But if you feel down, head for the gym. It can be a great outlet for repressed emotional anger – it releases a good rush of endorphins, and focuses your mind. A physical workout gives you mental strength, stability and confidence in yourself and the way you look and feel, and what could be better for your future dating prospects than a good mental and physical workout? (It gives you thinner thighs, too.) Oh, and it's easy to pull in a gym – see page 78 for tips.

Expressing your fears and negativity by writing a diary is another tried and tested cathartic solution. Identifying and listing your 'issues' is the first step to tackling them before they poison your next relationship. A word of caution, though! This diary needs a lock and cannot be shown to anyone else. Letting your next man find out about your bunny-rabbit-murdering tendencies is not a good move.

And whilst you're writing things down, don't forget to spend an afternoon listing all your ex's faults. Time erases all his most ghastly character traits which drove you round the bend at the time, and distance blows up and embellishes the positives out of all proportion. But the relationship ended, so it couldn't have been that good, could it? A long list of the things you hated about him is always good to refer to and helps you move on when doubts creep in.

Do all of these things. Get that ex out of your system. Ex-lovers are unworthy of your attention, so why poison your life with bitterness?

Even if, as you're reading all this, you're thinking you still get on with your ex so none of this is relevant, you need to take note nevertheless.

Are you friends with your ex? Why? I don't call mine. It's very rare that ex-lovers can be friends. Even if you stay in touch, you usually end up competing with each other to see who can move on first with the most fabulous new lover. You don't need this. *Drop him. The sooner you cut him out of your life, the better.* Emotionally it prevents you moving on, drains your energy and damages your soul. Every moment you waste dwelling on or staying in contact with the ex is a complete waste of time.

Oh, and if in a moment of hysterical madness you actually think of getting back with your ex (or just hopping into bed with him), then you must be insane. By doing that you're remaining in suspended animation in an emotional place you need to leave miles behind you.

There are too many good things to be had out there, and you'll never have enough time to experience them all if you stay hung up on the ex. Don't dwell on the past but dive into the glorious possibilities that the future holds.

Get rid of your baggage and move on!
No more if-onlys. No more regrets. Stop thinking, 'If I had done this or done that I could have saved my previous relationship from the rocks,' or, 'That was my only chance of happiness and I blew it,' or 'I'm too old and haggard/fat/busy/inherently evil, and totally jinxed with a dreadful personality to pull.'

It's high time to move on and climb out of the mindset that allows you to convince yourself that it is somehow your fault when relationships start to go pear-shaped. All of us have had bad relationships. You've had them. I've had them. (A guy once dumped me just because my house was haunted by a dead cat. Totally unreasonable!)

Never think you're 'jinxed' or have 'the black spot' on you. By doing that you're allowing the ghosts of exes to determine your life still. Learn what you need to from the experience and move on. (I just moved house so the spook pussy couldn't mess things up for me again.)

In a weird way you may actually end up being grateful to your ex, for learning from him will make your next relationship so much better.

No matter what the reasons are that you're single, deal with them and move on.

Epictetus, a Greek philosopher who was born in AD 55, used to say that humans don't get annoyed by actual events but by what they individually *think* about these events. What he meant was that if you can't change your world, your own reality, you can at least change the way you're thinking about it.

Eric Idle, who was born slightly later, reckoned in *Monty Python* that 'Life's a crock of sh*t', which is a bit negative, but his advice that you should just whistle and smile and get on with it anyway is good.

Don't dwell on the past, or not *allow* yourself to be happy. Trust me, this will just serve to make you angry when you look back and realise how much time you wasted by wallowing in your own self-doubt.

Always endeavour to see the lighter side of things. Try a bit of positive thinking and you'll find the world a much easier place to live in, and that includes dating! If you have time, try reading one of Deepak Chopra's books about spirituality. If not (there are around forty, and they cover things like quantum physics, which you may not be able to face before breakfast), then try and remember one of his tips, which is that every problem should be seen as a chance in disguise.

Your singledom problem is simply a chance to bag yourself a new, wonderful man.

The *mise en place* – or, get ready, girls!

'Beauty is in the eye of the beholder.'
PROVERB

And can really be helped with a few sit-ups, a lip wax,
a decent facial and a weekend session in a spa.

GERRY

Mise en place is the term masterchefs use to refer to the process of preparing ingredients long before they ever hit the saucepan – slicing the herbs, peeling potatoes, shelling the peas. All this has to be done with the utmost care, otherwise the ensuing dish will be utterly ruined!

In our case, girls, you, your bodies, wardrobes, minds, emotions and so on are our raw ingredients, and they'll have to be processed and directed in order to prepare this delectable dish – *you*. The dish at whom men will be literally throwing themselves, from left and right! Think of yourself as today's special on *Ready Steady Cook*.

Let's see what we need to get ready to win you the votes for dish of the day.

Your mind

I've put this first because getting into the right frame of mind before your dating campaign is crucial. There's no point turning up looking fabulous if you then sit in the corner sulking and doing a wallflower impression all night. The mind is the control base from which everything else takes its cue. In the same way that you slip your mind into crossword mode so that all your thoughts are directed towards deciphering clues and filling in the answers, your mind needs to be put into relationship-ready mode when it comes to dating.

Now, I know being single can often be hard, especially in a city where there's a lot of loneliness around. Listen – all of us have felt lonely at one time or another. It's a natural part of the human condition. The trick is not to let this loneliness lead to depression and maudlin thoughts, which in turn lead to fuzzy thinking where affairs of the heart are concerned. A lot of girls I talk to often blame themselves, think that they are somehow unworthy, and end up feeling defeated, crushed and small. And when you're feeling like that you can end up in unacceptable situations with men you don't fancy but go along with just for the company and the feeling that someone's taking an interest.

Sweeties, I can understand this behaviour. But I cannot allow it. It's mawkish (and probably downright sluttish!) Chin up (and knickers up too). If you're finding yourself in situations like these, you need to take yourself firmly in hand. (See it as training for the firm hand you'll later take with your boyfriend!) You're not unworthy. You're fabulous and you deserve to find someone fabulous. Remember this.

If you feel down, give yourself time every day to get centred, clear your mind of stress and have a few moments of being totally at peace with yourself. Go on, spoil yourself. See what works for you to make you feel good – and don't feel guilty. You might want to try exercise. Perhaps scented candles and meditation sessions in the bath with mating-whale sounds on the stereo. A friend of mine goes to Chanel (minus her purse) and tries

on every single style of shoe before leaving and ꞔ
announcing she prefers what they've got down th
in Prada.

Do whatever floats your boat. Train yourself nuc to
pay attention to the negative thoughts that crowd in
when you're tired or have had a stressful or horrible day.
That old saying that things will look better in the morning is always true. When I feel dreadful, I think of the
most beautiful place I can imagine – an island of blue
skies and blue seas, for example.

Each day, step out of the door with your head held
high and walk with the assurance of someone who is
master of all she surveys. If you don't feel it, fake it.

Girls, I implore you, please see yourselves as something wonderful. Tell yourself this every day. The most
important relationship of all is with yourself – you
should feel contented and at peace!

Don't even consider that you'll be refused anything,
and invariably you'll get what you want. Radiate pos-
itivity, project self-belief and confidence and men will
treat you that way.

Right then. Chins up? Blues banished? Let's move on
to the body.

Your body
Are you a bit … voluptuous? So what? Men like curvy,
Rubenesque women (within certain limits, of course!)
They don't necessarily want skinny-minnies (unless

they're David Beckham); they want J-Lo, with her
bouncy, curvy derrière! And that's not a new trend. Marilyn Monroe, the original bombshell, was allegedly a size
sixteen and men went mad for her. In fact, all the males
in my focus groups noted that curvier women always
seem to have far more interesting personalities as well.
Let's face it – whilst all the skinny ones are down at the
gym and working out their fat and cardio ratios, you
curvier types are probably down at the pub, having fun,
and chatting up men.

Besides, when you follow my rules, he won't be seeing
you with your clothes off for at least three months. By
that time he'll be so bewitched that a tiny bit of voluptu-
ousness here and there won't even be noticed!

So don't aim to copy those size-zero pop stars and

models. I've met a lot of them and, believe me, they're pretty unattractive in the flesh. They're not sexy. They look like young scrawny boys! One household figure I know actually goes to parties with sliced cucumber in her handbag to stop her eating the canapés. How dull! And I've seen others panicking over how many calories a vitamin tablet can hold. How neurotic! I've seen these tragic figures faint at parties and premieres because they've stayed away from food. How sad! All that time starving to get into their party frock and they spend the night unconscious in A&E.

On the other hand, don't put on *too* much weight, either. Yes, girls. It may hurt you to hear this but I did promise you tough love. I hate the slogan, 'I'm fat therefore there is more of me for him to love.' Being severely overweight is as unhealthy and unsexy as being anorexic and as thin as a bean.

It's also a form of self-sabotage. You're whacking yourself out of the game before it has even begun.

It's a vicious circle. Depression or loneliness can often lead to comfort eating. This translates into bad body condition; this drags your self-esteem down. This leads to scenes where you start shouting at the microwave to hurry up! But snap out of it. Think back to what I said about the mind. Your state of mind is reflected in your body. You may think it's harsh of me to say it, but do you actually want to become like a fridge – as soon as you open your mouth a light comes on?

I'm not saying don't eat chocolate. I'm not saying you can't have nice food and wine. But adopt a simple mantra if you want to keep those pounds off:

Breakfast like a king, lunch like a prince, and dine like a pauper.

Never mind fad diets. This is age-old advice, but it works. Those midnight binges could be responsible for your love handles. Respect and love your precious body and men will fall in love with it as well.

(And yes, I know I put on twelve kilos writing this book and I now have a tubby tummy, but that was an act of love and self-sacrifice for you. I'm going to the gym four times this week and I'm grilling some salmon as I write. These love handles will be gone in a month.)

On the subject of the body (oh, this is going to make me so unpopular, but you need telling), girls: some of my male friends do moan on about body hair. There are some men out there who are in pursuit of the hirsute, but the rest appreciate a smooth womanly surface, and not only on the legs and bikini line ...

Take a long look at yourself in the mirror under a bright light. Is there a moustache there? Dare I suggest spreading on a bit of Jolene, or a threading session, or electrolysis? (Look, Greek girls have to do this all the time. Even I go out and buy hair bleaching kits to cope with fuzzy bits. Fingers crossed, if this books goes well

I'm going in for a full-on laser hair massacre. It's perfectly normal – just do it.)

And do shave under the arms. I still shudder at the memory of Julia Roberts waving at everybody with those horror hairy armpits on the red carpet.

Okay, there are occasions when excess bodily hair is acceptable. Boudicca probably had hairy armpits, but then she was busy burning Colchester and leading an uprising of the tribes against the occupying forces of the Roman Empire. You, however, have no such excuse.

Your age

Do you think you're too old? On the shelf? Oh, stop it! Older is sexy! You've got more experience, and you know yourself better than you did ten years ago. I myself dreaded reaching thirty. Gay years are like dog years and I'd always been told that reaching thirty was the death of the homosexual. But in fact at thirty-one I'm in better condition both mentally and physically than ever before. I think of myself as being still eighteen years old, except that I've now got thirteen years' life experience added on.

You don't need to worry if you hit the big milestones – eighteen, twenty-one, thirty, forty, a hundred, without a man. Each time you're in a better position than you were before. Besides, although ageing is inevitable, growing up is optional. You don't need to start having blue rinses and putting a rug on your knees yet, you know. And you can always lie. Hide two years in your twenties, three in your thirties, and so on. By the time you're a century old nobody will argue when you say you're ninety. (Incidentally, when you tell a lie about your age, always look him straight in the eye. It makes you look honest.)

Your style
Once we've got the mind, the body and the tache sorted, we can tackle your wardrobe.

Firstly, scrutinise yourself in front of a mirror and decide what your most wonderful features are. What do you wish to emphasise and what do you wish to minimise? Pick out clothes that flatter and show your figure – perhaps a colour that brings out your eyes, or a cut that flatters the bust. A great trick is to pop round the designer stores, try on all their clothes and get advice from their super-helpful salesgirls – who are all on commission and think you're really going to buy that £500 top – then go and buy something similar from the high street.

Give yourself a few tweaks. Perhaps dress a bit 1950s pulp fiction. Why not be a bit of a 'bad girl' à la Betty Page (Google her if you haven't a clue who I'm referring to!)? Think of Sandra Dee in *Grease* – she changed from a sugary lollipop of a girl into a sleek biker-chick to ensnare her man. Underneath she was the same girl, but she'd undergone a few attitude and cosmetic tweaks.

I don't mean appear trussed up in a full-on corset, wielding a whip every time you go out the door. Just fox yourself up a bit.

No sluttiness, though, girls – the rule here is that we tease, we hint, but we don't put all the goods out on display. If you show cleavage, then please don't show leg. You're a fox, not a floozy.

Take some tips from Mother Nature. She adorns birds with brightly coloured feathers and shapes – this is the hook with which they can catch a mate. One piece of eccentric jewellery is always a good way of catching a male mate. It gives him something to talk to you about. But don't festoon yourself with hundreds of pieces or you'll look like one of those festival ships which sail into dock, all covered in fireworks and streamers, and you'll scare him.

Also, unless you're a Latino beauty like J-Lo, I'd also say no to huge gold hoop earrings or medallions. You'll just look like you've raided Argos. And no, absolutely *no*, to those huge gold rings with coins set in them. They're hideous on everybody and you'll never pull.

Your perfume

Invest in a lovely perfume. Try to avoid everything sold with a tacky celebrity endorsement on it. We're trying to be classy girls here, and you can hardly be an exotic, mysterious figure if you douse yourself in Eau de Jade Goody.

Coco Chanel, the doyenne of Paris fashion herself, said, 'A woman without perfume is a woman without future.' Get yourself an exotically perfumed future. Your perfume is your aura, your signature. It's another way to indulge his senses, another detail to remember you by.

Go for a classic, chic scent – not overpowering, but enough to definitely be remembered. (Do *not*, under any circumstances, choose something another woman in his life has been associated with. Perhaps winkle the information out surreptitiously by talking with him briefly about his favourite women's scents. You don't want him hankering after the ex every time you snuggle your perfumed neck up close.)

When you choose a perfume, don't try it on those silly little paper sticks the sales girls give out. Try it on your wrists, so it mixes with your own skin's scent and examine how it interacts and develops. Ask a friend's honest opinion, then, if you get the thumbs-up, stick with it. Make it your signature scent from now on, so it will be permanently associated in his brain with an image of you.

A dear friend, who is an incredibly sexy woman, told me that when she leaves her partner's flat, she sprays areas of his bed with her perfume. Her poor bloke is horribly allergic and sneezes all the time as a result, but every time he closes his eyes in bed when he's alone, he's thinking of her.

A nice little trick is to buy a small atomiser spray, fill it with your perfume and, when you're on a date, spray behind the ears and on the wrists in front of him. Tilt your head backwards and expose your neck, and let him watch as you point the underside of your wrist towards him. In both these areas the skin is delicate and sensitive, and he will subconsciously interpret this as a submissive act from little old you to his big old powerful masculinity. (Silly, misguided fool! Of course, one of the basic premises of 'treating him mean' is that you can constantly play seductive games without him ever realising it.)

Make-up and pampering

I wear make-up myself – it hides a million imperfections. I believe no lady should leave her residence without powder and lipstick in her bag. When you're tired, a quick brush of bronzing powder livens your tone. (I use MAC bronzing powder – slightly expensive, but it'll last you for ages. Or Body Shop does cheaper versions.) Huge under-eye shadow horrors can be hidden by Yves Saint Laurent's Touche Éclat – all models use this. Some use it all over their faces, actually, but whilst that may work okay on cleverly lit photo-shoots, it can

make you look a little too luminous in the flesh.

Find a good foundation. Go to a posh department store and a sales person will show you the best shade for your skin. Fix it with a translucent powder and it will stay there all night. After sunset, wear a killer dark-shade lipstick if it suits you – but for daytime use lip balm or lighter glosses. They're less obvious but will still make him want to kiss your lips. (Don't overdo it though, and smear on loads – it will look like you've just eaten particularly oily sardines.) Last but not least, apply mascara. Here I must say thank you to my fellow inmate in the Big Brother madhouse – Lea. She tested twenty mascara brands for me for this book, so we can advise you of the best for peepers power. The one she thinks is brilliant, and separates eyelashes without smudging, is Maybelline's Define-A-Lash mascara. Happily that's one of the cheapest, too. Thanks, Lea, and happy eyelash fluttering, darling!

Never be scared to indulge and pamper yourself. A monthly salon visit. A spa evening if you can. Yes, it costs, but it's all an excellent investment of your time and money because if you look after yourself, you'll attract the same type of men.

And finally …

Don't believe the hype. Never feel insecure about not doing as well as other women.

Magazines are full of features about bionic women with four children, wonderful husbands and a spotless gigantic house bursting with antiques and handmade crystal chandeliers from Murano. They're pampered with the latest spa treatments, clad head-to-toe in exclusive Bond Street labels, they're cellulite-free, and they all have phenomenally successful careers in finance, fashion or PR.

I've met these women. I assure you – they're mummified with Botox, have lizard-skin necks from all those expensive holidays in the sun, enjoy hourly breakdowns with their children and go nuts with insecurity every time their perfect husband comes within reach of a woman half their age. Oh, and they also have cellulite. Everyone does.

Love yourself, and it will be the beginning of a life-long romance. Vanity is not such a bad thing when it makes you assertive as well as stylish. One of the most fabulous women that ever lived, Madame de Pompadour, had the French king following her every whim … and was incredibly vain. It is said that when Madame de Pompadour lay dying, she called out to God, 'Wait a second,' and dabbed her cheeks with rouge!

Now then, one final checklist to approve our *mise en place*. I want a full set of ticks:

- ✓ Positive attitude in place?
- ✓ Kitten heels on?
- ✓ Whiskers dealt with?
- ✓ Best frock on?
- ✓ Massive hold-it-all-in-knickers-to-create-illusion-of-perfect-figure on underneath?
- ✓ Lip gloss on?
- ✓ Handbag packed with lipstick, powder, perfume and paint?

You're now ready to devour that new man you've had your eye on!

Prove to your collection of ex-lovers and boyfriends that you are *so* over them, and bag the perfect man. It doesn't matter if it takes some time. The slower vengeance ripens, the sweeter it is when it is plucked!

And don't forget to enjoy your man-free freedom right now. It's actually great that you're single again – or if you prefer it, 'between boyfriends'. Great because you can have all the fun of dating and meeting Mr Right. Now, read my tips, and go out and get plucked!

Your dating black book

If you want to get the juiciest boy worms out there, then you have to approach dating in the same way that you approach the January sales – with determination, ruthlessness, pre-planning and a list. The only difference between sale shopping and men shopping is that you can do the former in flat heels – but I demand at least four inches for the latter.

GERRY

Get yourself a little black book (or maybe not so little – I'm going to make you a man magnet) and use it to plan your attack. If you meet men you like, write down their names and plot their course over the succeeding weeks. Where did you meet? Did you flirt? Did they call? Note it down! How long did it take them to call? Note it down! Where was the first date, what were his good and bad points, was he keen, did he propose … you get the idea. Make a shortlist of the men you're interested in and why. Record the places or social functions you met men and make it a priority to visit them again. It's good to have a list of good man spots that you can refer back to whenever there's a drought.

Ignore those people who say you'll find love when you're not looking for it. Rubbish! Go looking! Put the same amount of focus on finding a man as you do on your career. Why not? You're usually in a relationship far longer than you are in a job, so you should approach boyfriend searching with the same seriousness and planning as job hunting!

Before starting the search (or hunt!), its essential to know exactly what you want and what you have to offer. Please fill in the following charts. Come on! Nobody's watching! Pretend you're looking for a new job. You can't just go out there willy-nilly looking for anything. You need to focus on your strengths, your needs and what you can put up with on a daily basis.

Be totally honest, please!

This simple exercise will help you recognise your personal strengths and face up to any negatives that you perhaps shy away from.

Take a deep breath and look clearly and bravely at your weaknesses. This will help you focus on things you might need to address about your personality, appearance or habits.

My positives	My negatives
Come on, there must be something. Ask your friends for their tips. Are you loyal? Patient? Funny? Can you make soufflés? Can you fake an interest in football? Can you fake an orgasm?	*Now then, be honest. Are you a lousy cook – do your soufflés sink? Are you a touch impatient? Have you featured on a documentary entitled:* Girlfriends from Hell?

Your wish list

Now let's do a list of potential men. Make a wish list of your dating 'must-haves' (but, of course, don't ever talk about them to your suitors). These could be appearance, success in the workplace, well spoken, manners, sexual prowess. (Hussy! Not that you'll be finding out about that until the relationship is well down the garden path!)

As you start the actual dating, score each man you're

seeing against this little table of yours in your black book. But do be realistic! For instance, 'He must be able to drive' is fine, but, 'He must drive a Ferrari' is a teensy bit overambitious! Don't waste time and tears throwing yourself at unattainable men (catwalk models, pop stars, world leaders). We are indeed playing for high stakes, but this is no James Bond movie. (Anyway, James Bond may be good in bed but he's utterly rubbish at commitment, so shy away from him and his type like the plague, girls!)

		Yes	No
Age	**Can you bear an age-gap relationship?** (I only mean a couple of years mind – no cradle-snatching, please. And we want a man driving a nice car not a Zimmer.)		
Personality	**What are the most important qualities you're looking for:** Sensitive? Funny? Articulate? Mature? Down-to-earth? Protective? Romantic? Masculine? Absolutely loaded?		

		Yes	No
Looks	**Height** (Are you tall? Could you bear life in flats with a shorter man? Carla Bruni still looks ravishing in them ...) **Hair** (Does he have to have some? Do you mind dyed hair? Remember black hair dye can play havoc with white bedlinen.) **Do you mind dating a larger-build man?** (Remember – he will make you look thinner.) **Do you mind a hairy back?** (Do remember you're unlikely to find a perfect 10, so maybe allow a few faults and aim for a 7.) **List your absolute no-nos:**		
Employ-ment	**Do you want Mr Career Man?** **Can you cope with the bohemian life of a penniless artist?**		
Financial status	**Could you date a man who earns less than you?** **Do you want one that earns more?** (You little gold-digger!)		

		Yes	No
Education	Does education matter to you? Must a man have made it through: Secondary school? Diploma? Degree? Masters? Ph.D.? Is the University of Life enough?		
Child-raising potential	Do you want children? Do you have children?		
Interests and hobbies	Do they need to match yours? Must he be into: Cinema? Travel? Music? Eating out? Cooking? Cycling? Cars? Palaeontology? Saving the world?		
Fitness	Does he need to be a gym bunny?		
Habits	Could you date a smoker?		
House ownership	Be honest! I don't mind helping out the gold-diggers amongst you. Do you not want to get attached unless he's got at least a semi-detached?		

These points will give you ideas of where to hunt for your man as you read through my book. Need a career man? Then use the dating tips for bars near where offices are (page 79). Don't mind a smoker? Head for the smoking areas and follow my tips on smirting (page 81). Need a six-pack? Cut to the tips on pulling in the gym (page 78). Need an educated man? There are dating sites on the Internet where you can post education wish lists. I've got Internet flirting tips coming up too (page 114). Want a man with cash? Well, good for you, why shouldn't you want a man who can afford to spoil you and drip diamonds over you? I'm all for going on the hunt for a rich man, and for you little lovelorn gold-diggers, there are tips on making sure you avoid students and penniless bohemian types (page 84).

But don't be too rigid. Don't load your 'shopping list' with unrealistic expectations. Okay Angelina Jolie, found her Brad Pitt, but then she's a world famous and extremely rich movie star with a ridiculously sexy mouth. Us mere mortals without bee-stung lips can't all wander round with a Brad Pittometer in our heads rejecting all who don't reach impossibly high standards. I'm not asking you to date the local hunchback, but there's a lot to be said for giving men who aren't physically faultless a bit of a chance. Perfect tens are hard to find. Maybe give a guy who is a seven in the looks and status stakes a second look?

Too many women have a blueprint in their mind of

what their man should look like. They've decided exactly how he'll dress his gorgeous six-foot-three frame, and how he'll gaze at them with his perfect blue eyes as they run their fingers through his thick, sun-bleached hair. Then along comes a perfectly decent man who asks them on a date, and he gets rejected because he doesn't match up to all these ideals.

Girls, keeping a blueprint in your head and sticking to it rigidly is just daft. Don't let real-life men go because they don't match up to Mr Imaginary. You may be murdering budding wonderful relationships before they've even had the chance to commence.

Let me tell you about hunky-looking men. An exceptionally gorgeous guy may seem like a catch, but he probably isn't. If men are physically gorgeous, they will always be able to rely on their tall frame and good looks. They don't need to put effort into developing an arresting personality or begin to understand how to keep a woman happy. And, oh my God these sorts of men are high-maintenance. I know because I've dated some of them. That gorgeous chest will need waxing, that tan will need hours of fake baking in salons, perfect skin needs constant facials and those thighs demand hours in a gym. How dull!

Remember, looks fade, six-packs have an expiry date (my poor six-pack expired last year, God rest its soul), but brains and personality last much longer. If someone you like asks you out, but he doesn't quite fit your preconceptions of how your partner will look, don't turn him down flat. Give him a chance. Go on a date. If you don't like him, then fine, move on. It's only one evening, and at the very worst you'll perhaps gain a friend, which can hardly be a bad thing!

And don't dismiss someone because they don't have a wildly exciting job, either. Hot totty exists in the unlikeliest places. There are some wonderful physical specimens in my gym who tell me they work in the IT department; and, trust me, when my Edinburgh flat was burning, the firemen that came round were all, sadly, pretty ugly. (The cute ones were probably busy oiling themselves in anticipation for the annual charity calendar photo-shoot.)

Here's a case study to illustrate the perils of being too picky.

Kate, 33

As the youngest child with three older siblings all happily married, Kate had exceptionally high standards. She had just come out of a very bad relationship. She went out with a man who ticked all the boxes of her 'blueprint man', he was dark, tall and handsome and financially well off. But he was also a serial cheater and was so arrogant that he didn't even bother to hide it, leaving her emotionally scarred.

After one year, she met Tom in a bar. He was precisely the opposite of her blueprint 'ideal' man.

With some misgivings, she accepted a first date and things got off to a very successful start, but she was still unsure and held back because his appearance didn't match her blueprint. By chance she saw her 'gorgeous' ex one evening, and all the horror of their relationship came flooding back, forcing her to re-evaluate her stance and give this new man a chance. 'Tom was scruffy but strong. Certainly not stunning, but definitely caring. I felt secure for the first time in years.'

Last year I was invited to their wedding, and they have now been together for six years. Kate is pregnant, and Tom is destined to make a great parent.

So come on. Give that Mr Ordinary a chance. He may turn out to be Mr Perfect after all.

Choose the target, play the game!

Now you've got rid of your old baggage and worked out what you're looking for in a boyfriend or relationship, it's time to learn a few basic rules of the dating game.

And yes, it *is* a game, with strategies and tricks, as well as some rules, to make sure you win every time …

PART TWO

How To Treat Him Mean
When You Meet Him

'Mens sana in corpore sano.'
(A healthy mind in a healthy body.)

That's what we want, girls. Not *mens insana* in your
hideous tracksuit bottoms moping at home.

GERRY

Okay. That's enough analysis. We're running out of time. All the best-looking men are getting snapped up. I need you to get out there.

I've always despised ultimatums, but they do seem to work. You have needlessly been single for far too long! Imagine it's five minutes before midnight on a Friday and you must take drastic action *now*. Change your fate, before the cruel years pass and you become a lonely, blue-rinsed OAP stuck in singledom limbo indefinitely!

Aux armes mes filles! Rise to the challenge! I know I probably sound like Lenin addressing a May-Day rally in Red Square consisting of thousands of synchronised tanks and marching bands. But I do take my role as your date coach very seriously. I feel it's my duty to put a metaphorical firecracker up your caboose and wake up any of you who have slipped into an unhealthy slumber of self-pity.

There's no point sitting at home. Those men won't come round and start battering the door down, and if they did, in your present state they would probably find you with mascara smeared across the top half of your face and Häagen-Dazs across the bottom half.

Get off your behind! Your Mr Darcy is out there, but he's not coming to you, so don't wait for him. Let's start teaching you the lessons of the dating game, my little ponirias.

Be bad

Lesson one is that you must be bad. You must be ruthless.

Do you sometimes feel overlooked by guys in favour of girls more determined and predatory than you? Or, horror of horrors, have you propositioned a guy you fancied and had him reply with the classic: 'You're a really nice girl, but I just don't see you in that way!'? What a crusher. How *does* he see you, then? Does he think you're Julie Andrews?

So what have you been doing wrong?

You must have heard many women saying that're attracted to 'bad boys', and, whilst I don't approve of bad boys, you should take this little titbit on board. Be a bad girl. There's no point sitting there with big puppy-dog eyes doing your Mary Poppins act and waiting for him to notice you. What's the point of holding off, giving him flirting signals until he knows you so well that he sees you as a sister figure?

You should start giving out alluring but discreet 'I fancy you' vibes from the *moment* you meet him. You need to show him early on that you're into him. The only way to uproot a nettle is to grab it *firmly*. Pussyfoot about and you'll get stung! Sweethearts, we simply can't waste time if we're going to get you that man and the sparkling diamonds you deserve.

Be ruthless. Divide your world into two types of men – those you can date and those who are friends. Be really, really nice to your friends. And let the other men be really, really nice to you.

Don't believe me? Still say you shouldn't play games? Here's a case study to illustrate:

Cara and Lauren

Cara and Lauren were housemates in their late twenties, but unfortunately they secretly despised each other. The reason? Cara was playing games with her men. She was what we call a bad girl. And lo and behold, the men came flocking to her door! Lauren always asked herself: 'Why do they fall for her the way she treats them? I'm a nice, honest human being and not into these sorts of games.'

Needless to say, Lauren is still single whilst Cara is now married.

What Lauren has done is miss the point. Instead of being jealous of Cara, she should have been hanging on to her every word and pumping her for details about how to engineer the same type of success. Cara was ultimately the more honest of the two, if not always the most likeable. At least she knew what she wanted and was determined to get it, and had the drive to go for it!

Poor Lauren, on the other hand, was jealous of her success. She tried to delude herself into thinking that it was because she was too 'nice' and 'honest' and 'didn't play games' that she couldn't get a man. What rubbish! Lauren is still single because she was flumped on the sofa waiting for men to call, and tutting at Cara's behaviour when she should have been joining her, steaming out of the door dressed to kill.

To be good at dating, you need to be a bit of a bad girl. I'm not asking you to become Cruella De Vil and go killing his puppies, just to sharpen it up a bit. These games we play are designed to get us a man and to keep him keen once we've got him.

Be a fox and outsmart the competition! Machiavelli in *The Prince* advises you to be a fox and not a lion. The lion falls into traps because, though it's courageous, it's also presumptuous in that it doesn't spy out the terrain properly beforehand and relies too much on its strong persona without doing its homework. In contrast, the fox sniffs out a good opportunity but makes damn sure to check out the terrain and pitfalls before going in for the kill.

Remember, we don't have the advantage of being able to sit at debutante balls waiting to be chosen, or getting a maiden aunt to do the running for us any more. You need to be more proactive. You need to stop being so nice or you won't get your man. Nobody ever liked that nice-as-apple-pie Janet Weiss in *The Rocky Hor-*

ror Show. Even her husband cheated on her with a mad transvestite.

Be competitive! Step out of your comfort zone. This is no time for being a shrinking violet. You're going to have to network and hobnob in a very determined way. Bear in mind you've just bought a lovely black diary to fill. If you stay glued to your seat in a bar and switched to mute all night, you won't have anything to fill it with, which would be a pity both for it and for you!

How to flirt – and where

'A woman is like a tea-bag; you never know how strong she is until you put her in hot water.'
ELEANOR ROOSEVELT

I know it's scary to talk to men, but always remember these wise words. Get out there, my little PG Tipsters, and plunge into the hot water of the dating world!

GERRY

Let's start filling in that little black book. To meet the right men you have to go to the right places. After all, if you were going out deerstalking, you wouldn't park yourself in a shopping mall or bowling alley with a shot-gun, would you? It's important to know where to stalk your man.

I'm sick of hearing girls saying they never meet men.

Do you live in a nunnery or something? The world is full of them.

Here's a list of places you can go to stalk your prey.

The gym
In the modern metropolis there exists a type of man who doesn't have much time for the social scene. He's very aware of his fitness levels, adds aminos and creatine to his protein shake, and assesses his body-fat ratio monthly. Gym bunnies may sound a tad obsessive or even boring, but remember, they look fit, will age well and most importantly, can perform in bed for longer! (Sex is a cardio exercise, after all.) Now, which ones to target? Easy. The ones looking at each other are the gay ones. The ones looking at themselves flexing in the mirror like peacocks are the narcissists. Go for all the rest.

Observe his weekly timetable – first thing in the morning, lunch break, after work etc.) and make sure you go to the gym on the same days.

The water fountain is the gym's man trap. Watch over him and suddenly get thirsty at exactly the same time. Think of something to say – 'Having a good workout?' And smile.

My friend Eve, a sexy dental nurse, met her (sadly now ex) boyfriend by asking instructions on how to work out on a particular weights machine. He will feel wonderfully flattered that you've selected him as your personal trainer. Fitness instructors hold a certain sexual prestige within the gym environment, since female clients pay them a huge amount of attention that other men in the gym always kind of envy. I highly recommend the lat pull-down machine (back exercises). He will have to position himself behind you to help, and he'll get a lovely flattering sneak-peek of your décolleté area. Alternatively, simply ask him, 'Could you please pass me that towel?' The one that you've 'accidentally' just left in his training area. You little minx!

Cocktail and wine bars

Your entrance into a bar is everything. (You're the flame and the men are the moths. Okay, you don't want to attract B-movie men-insects, but you get the analogy.)

If you suffer from lack of confidence when you walk into a bar, then practise this technique. Imagine yourself walking into an awards ceremony. Red carpet, long Donna Karan dress, strappy sandals. Imagine Oscars. Keep that picture in your head and replay it as you walk into a bar with your head held high. Many athletes use this technique when they're preparing for an important event. If you're a sprinter, you see yourself running the final three metres as a winner. Use the same technique to imagine yourself walking into a bar as a man-magnetising stunner.

Find your object of desire (check for a lack of wedding band first, ladies!), and then watch for when he goes to the bar. Follow him. Stand near him. And then smile nicely, hand him a tenner and ask if he could possibly get your drink in when he orders his round?

Now, perhaps it is a bit devious doing all the girlie 'I'm too small and weak to push through this crowd to the bar because I'm a lady' act. But it works. He'll enjoy this. You're making him feel all big, strong and clever because he can get the barman's attention whilst little old you can't.

And do order a ladylike drink, girls. A charming smile and request for a kir royal is perfect. (Occasionally the barman is new and will have no clue, at which point you clarify – simply champagne plus a drizzle of crème de cassis in a flute – which makes you sound sophisticated and knowledgeable. Ordering a pint of lager misses the point.)

This technique will get his attention, and by the time he hands you the drink, there will have been a million opportunities for small talk.

But do offer to pay, girls, or this won't work. You're asking the big strong man to get in the queue for you, not begging him for a freebie. Do it this way and it's the modern-day equivalent of the medieval technique of dropping a handkerchief for a man to pick up. Do it by asking for a free drink and it's the equivalent of dropping your knickers.

Smoking areas
I hate smoking, but it's a very useful pulling tool.

Smoking areas can be the best place to find a man. Going 'smirting' (smoking/flirting) is great fun. Everyone is relaxed. They're penned into one area so there's easy access. You can see what they really look like outside the club's flattering lighting, and you don't have to shout over the music. Smokers are also relaxed when they're in the smoking area. They'll all be chatting to each other and there'll be no pushing and shoving like there is inside a club. You can also choose your victim at the bar and simply follow him outside every half-hour without looking like a mad stalker.

You don't even have to smoke to go smirting. I've given up smoking, but I'm still a regular in the smoking area outside Mahiki nightclub. It's the best place in the club.

(Having said that, smoking is disgusting, so try and find a smoker who keeps saying he wants to give up.)

This technique only really works in summer. It's no fun in the winter when it's snowing.

Run a Flirtathon. Not a Drinkathon.
When you're hunting, you need to be in control!

Parties

A mischievous lady I went to university with (now settled with kids – she knows who she is) had an innovative way of attracting attention at a party. She would target the party bore – some unfortunate chubby-cheeks nerd who I hope by now is a software colossus – and strike up a long conversation with him. When she saw the object of her desire passing, she would whisper in a conspiratorial tone to him, 'Save me, Save me, please!' Tremendously shallow, but it worked every time.

Hotel bars

Don't limit your search to local men – try out-of-towners too. Women in the know recommend hotel bars as excellent spots to meet them.

Ask that charming man, 'You're not from London/Manchester/Llanfairpwllgwyngyllgogerychwyrndrobwyll-llantysiliogogogoch?' If they reply 'Yes', you hit them with 'How come I haven't met you before?' If they reply 'No', you comment, 'I didn't think so. If you were I would have met you by now!'

As in any busy hunting ground, don't stay in one spot all night – circulate. You can always pretend you're looking for an imaginary friend who's late.

Running clubs

Like the athletic type? Join a running club, girls! This is a surefire way of getting yourself a healthy guy, too. You can check his stamina as he does his circuit training (and his six-pack too!)

Tie your hair back, whack on a little waterproof

mascara and go for the fresh-faced sporty look. Invest in some sexy black lycra to complete the effect. Lycra is a wonderfully flattering fabric on a woman. It's almost like wearing a corset. It lifts, flattens and enhances curves. Plus it stops everything flopping about whilst you run around.

Search on the Internet – there are ex-army guys who run outdoor exercise sessions for men and women throughout the UK. If you don't pull, you'll still get to flirt with soldiers and tone up. There are absolute beginners' classes around, so even if you're a touch on the voluptuous side, there's bound to be someone bigger than you. Plus you're getting a workout whilst you look out for men, so you're getting more toned and better-looking by the second.

Of course, if you can't be bothered with all the exercise, or if exercise leaves you hot, sweaty and bright red, then just fake it. A good friend of mine merely turns up at the London marathon each year in a running top and follows the best-looking runners to the pub once they've finished.

Museums and galleries
These are fabulous places to pull. You'll find a very up-market man here. Business men. Refined men. I once met a wonderful American guy in a gallery.

I know some of you are after a man of substance, though. If the size of a man's bank balance is top of the list for you, then do be careful, as there are also a lot of skint students in there who are just sheltering there to stay warm, and I'd hate for you to waste your time.

Go for auction house sale previews if you want to meet men with money – then you can be assured that at least some of the men are there because they're looking to buy.

A word of warning about artists. Artists are lovely, lovely people, but they do have a tendency to sit around for decades waiting to be discovered. If you like your material things, then their bohemian lifestyle may well drive you crazy. If you really can't bear dating a man who earns less than you, an easy way to judge how successful an artist is is to ask them if they've had a solo exhibition. If an artist has not had a solo exhibition by the age of twenty-six, go to the next gallery, my little money-grabbers. This man will never make it.

Trains and tubes

We live in a commuting culture, and, alas, we spend a big percentage of our lives on public transport. Use it!

It's a lot easier to pull on public transport in the north of England because everyone there talks to each other. In the south I've found it's different. But there are some techniques you can try, and they are great ways of livening up some very long, dull commutes.

If it's your daily commute then take your time. Don't rush in on day one yelling your phone number over the ticket barrier. People tend to take the same train every day and sit in the same place, so play it cool. Just get there a couple of minutes earlier each day to make sure you can bag your place right next to Mr Wonderful.

Give out signals from day one, but do it subtly as you gradually build a net to catch that little fishy prey. Smile at him one day. Say 'good morning' the next. Comment on the weather twenty-four hours later. After a week, drop something on the floor – a book or mobile phone. Does he pick it up for you? If nothing else, flirting like this livens up the journeys and puts a spring in your step.

On the tube you can take more risks, as you may never see the same person at the same station again. Break the rules a little and be a bit more forward. Smile. Start a conversation. Ask for directions. Say anything at all – just start talking.

Be brave. Think *Brief Encounter*. Nothing ventured, nothing gained. Don't worry, if you make a complete mess of it all and get a flat knock-back, you can simply set off five minutes earlier in the morning, sit in a different carriage, or take the bus to work instead and you'll never see him again.

Everywhere else
Look, there are a million opportunities to flirt. Don't worry, just do it!

I pulled a man at a bus stop once. I smiled and told him he looked just like my friend Brian. Actually, I don't know anyone called Brian, but it still worked a treat.

In a DVD shop you can comment on his choice: 'What a great choice! I've seen this movie twenty times and I adore it.' In a record shop tell him it's a 'classic album. I went to their gig last summer!' Okay, you have no clue what you're talking about – but he hasn't, either, because he hasn't bought it yet. Bluff your way into a conversation. Even if he doesn't ask you for a coffee, it's all practice.

The more pieces of bait you drop into the water, the more dates you get, and the more chances to catch a great big fish.

Like I said, approach dating the same way you approach work. If you sent off a CV and didn't get a job, you wouldn't give up and assume you were unemployable, would you? No. You'd keep trying. So keep sending out those flirting signs. You'll soon see the rewards. Just get yourself out there.

How to flirt when you're out with the girls

'If you want to go quickly, go on your own.
If you want to go far, go together.'
OLD PROVERB

Just make sure you pick the right fellow hyenas
to go out hunting with.
GERRY

The last chapter was all about how to hunt solo as a lonely wolf. But going out with the girls and hunting as a pack is also great fun. Just make sure you pick a good wingwoman.

Hunting with the girls is best done with between one and three other females. A larger number of wingwomen is more difficult to keep in control and you might end up looking like man-eating hyenas.

But who do you choose as your vital, man-chasing sidekick? Some books advocate that you only go out with women who are less attractive than you so that you shine. This may be quite tempting, but I completely disagree. If you're out in a bar with Ugly Betty, then men are simply not going to come to you. If you only hang out with women who are much fatter than you, then men will not look over and see you looking thin and fabulous by comparison. They'll just see a bunch of fat women. Men can also take it as a sign of insecurity if you've surrounded yourself with a bunch of ugly people to make yourself feel better. Take a look at Hollywood and showbiz people out on the town – they've often surrounded themselves with these short, hefty, dumpy people so they get all the attention.

Personally I think you should go out with those friends who are funny, charismatic, beautiful and who you love spending time with. They'll lift you up. You'll benefit from their aura. Go out with girls who make you feel good. You should all be motivating and encouraging each other. If you feel insecure, perhaps invite your married and attached friends along to be your wingwomen. They can help you hunt, but won't be in competition for the men.

I don't know your friends and I'm sure they're all wonderful, but do be ruthless when it comes to choosing a wingwoman who'll make you feel good. The problem is that girls can sometimes – deliberately or not – scupper each other's chances.

Let me give you examples of bad wingwomen:

The one that dredges up your past:
Does she put you down in front of a man? Does she dredge up tales from your childhood, telling the man: 'Oh, remember when you were drunk and you were vomiting …' Do you feel uncomfortable sometimes when you're with her? She may be using your past experiences to tell a joke, but it's not funny if you're the

punchline. Ditch her and go with a girl who always puts you in a good light.

The slutty one:
Beware of a wingwoman who wears embarrassingly inappropriate attire – the mini is too mini, the make-up is clownish. You'll look slutty by association.

The one that needs constant attention:
Does she require endless babysitting when you need a few minutes of space to work your magic on your catch? Does she get drunk too easily and do you end up having to look after her before she starts snogging the local Quasimodo? Is she antagonistic or does she act as an emotional barrier between you and your man, interrupting your conversation all the time to talk about herself? If you've got to spend all night looking after her needs, you'll never look after your own.

Dump these girls. You'll never pull with wingwomen like these.

An ideal wingwoman is there to help you pull. You choose your prey. She should respect your choice. Her job is to initiate conversation with him and then introduce the gorgeous you. Your prey will have dropped his guard because the wingwoman has made you appear less predatory, more charming and relaxed. As you flirt away with him, the perfect wingwoman should then go on to distract the target's (sometimes less desirable) companion to give you time to reel in your prey.

Of course, when the moment comes, you must repay the favour. If your wingwoman has her eye on someone later on, you must offer the same level of assistance. And be as willing to chat up his ugly mate.

We've spotted our prey. What do we do to get that date?

The art of body language

'I speak two languages, Body and English.'
MAE WEST

Okay, let's teach you a few key phrases in both.
GERRY

If you haven't got a wingwoman to go off and get men for you, you can always lure men in with body language.

Every great seductress needs a sophisticated arsenal of body-language moves. With practice, you can scan a room for your prey, find out if he's interested in you, lure him over and let him know you're a hot little lover. All without saying a word. Here's how to drop the bait.

The eyes
Across a busy environment, lock your gaze on him for

five seconds or so and then look away. Then look again, bat your eyelashes and say to him with your eyes, 'Hello, handsome, you are gorgeous!' Or even 'I am probably the best thing that has happened to you in a long time. Come and get me!'

Yes, you can say all this with your eyes, and if you don't believe me, practise in front of a mirror. Visualise your ideal man in front of you and imagine transmitting messages to him through your eyes. Study how your gaze can be playful and flirty with just a slight arching of your eyebrows and flutter of the eyelashes!

Don't be discouraged if he doesn't get the signal the first time. Experts calculate that a female has to repeat this courting process an average three times for the male to perceive it. (Yes, we men really are that slow.)

Of course, if you've spent an hour flashing 'come and get me' with your peepers across the bar and he still hasn't popped over, it's time to give up and move on.

The smile
All this fluttering of eyelashes will only be 100 per cent successful if you accompany it with a warm, playful smile.

At this point it's important to demonstrate the difference between a genuine and a fake smile:

- A genuine smile contracts the muscle group around the eyes named the orbicularis oculi (these, alas, also cause the so-called 'crow's feet'). These muscles pull back the eyes as well as the mouth.

- A phoney or 'plastic' smile can be encountered behind the perfumery desk of major department stores or on late-night TV shopping channels. It only involves the mouth, it looks like a clownish exaggerated grimace, and it will scare men away.

So, back to that mirror again. Practise faking that genuine smile so it reaches your eyes.

The mouth

Draw his attention to your mouth. Lick your lips. (Be careful to make this look sensual, though, not pornographic. It should seem like a quick, subconscious movement, not like you're standing there staring and slavering over him like a dog.) A good trick, which looks a bit more innocent, is to bite your lower lip or apply lipstick when you know he's watching you. This is the perfect excuse for prolonged pouting and draws further attention to your mouth. Get yourself a pretty mirror compact that you're proud to whip out in public, and apply away. Of course, another advantage of a mirror is that you can do a quick check behind you as you apply to see if any cute men are checking *you* out from behind.

Touching
Run a finger through your hair, then flick your hair away from your neck. Slowly move that finger from your ear-lobes towards your throat. Alternatively, stroke your arms just below the elbow. If you're sitting down, lay your arms on top of your thighs and slowly move them upwards as if lifting an invisible silk skirt.

Slowly remove one layer of clothing, like a jacket or even a silk scarf, while looking at him across a busy place. That should be perceived as an inviting gesture that you're ready to remove more for him. (Although, of course, you won't be. Not at this early stage!)

All these moves are very inviting, and any self-respect-ing straight man will automatically imagine doing those moves to you himself.

Do be subtle, though. Do just one move – don't sit there stroking yourself and undressing like a one-woman porn show. Practise in front of a mirror.

The side-glance
Lower one shoulder, tilt your head, and look upwards and sideways behind your exposed neck. A little back-wards glance over your shoulder as you leave the room works wonders. Marilyn Monroe did this all the time. Remember that playful smile!

The feet

I have asked hundreds of men what attracts them most about a woman. The most common answer is 'legs'. So use your legs. Use your feet. Point your feet towards him. If you're sitting in a bar, you can cross and uncross your feet as you talk, risking a little flash of thigh. Again, be subtle. Think flirty. Not hooker. Not Sharon Stone.

And wear heels. No matter how tall you are, wear heels. Never go to a cocktail bar in flats, for goodness' sake. Heels elongate the legs, make your calves look fabulous, and force your body into a sexy position. You have no idea how lucky you are to be able to wear them. There are lots of short men out there who'd kill for the chance of an extra four inches. If your feet hurt in heels, cheat and buy some of those 'party feet' gel inserts. They enable you to go on twice as long. All the models, celebs and heel-wearing slutties that I know wear them. You can even buy glitter ones.

Mirroring

This is another surefire technique that works on a sub-conscious level. When you talk to a man, discreetly duplicate his moves – mirror his posture, his facial gestures, the positioning of his arms. When he drinks, you sip from your glass. This courtship gesture creates an invisible bond because you're now tuning into his own body language. Keep it very low key, though; there's a thin line between that and making him think you're taking the mickey.

Posture

Be aware of your posture. Stand straight and upright, shoulder blades positioned backwards, torso extended. This way you'll avoid similarities with the hunchback of Notre-Dame, and it will also make your bust look fabulous. If friends have mentioned bad posture to you and it's a chronic problem, I couldn't recommend anything better than a weekly class of Pilates. Check local gyms or community centres. In only a few weeks with a good instructor, these sets of exercises will reposition your vertebrae and correct your posture.

Perfecting your body language is a never-ending exercise. Learn to enjoy being the centre of attention by using all these great tricks, even when you're in a relationship. Your partner will desire you more because you appear to be desired by other men. Improve these skills further by watching the interactions of people that surround you. Analyse how irresistible women flirt, how men respond and the spellbinding mating 'dance' that follows. Turn off the sound on the television and try to guess what the situation you're watching is about. Observe the gestures

and facial expressions of actors, especially during flirty/
erotic movie scenes.

'All right, Mr DeMille, I'm ready for my close-up.'

Is he interested?

Okay, so is it all working? If the object of interest is re-
ceptive to your signals he'll do the following:

- He'll establish eye contact and search the room
  for your gaze.
- Like a male bird preening his bright feathers at
  the sight of a female, he'll react by expanding
  his chest, adjusting his tie, rearranging his clothing,
  and dusting off his jacket.
- He'll imitate your moves, doing the mirroring
  technique just like you.
- He might demonstrate his interest by penis display.
  Don't panic, I don't mean he'll strip naked – I mean
  that without realising it he'll start trying to draw at
  tention to his crotch. He might start pointing his bits
  in your direction. If he's standing, he may protrude his
  hip bone or rest his thumbs on his belt, pointing his
  hands towards his crotch. If seated, he might simply
  spread his legs a bit. Yes, it's all rather primeval, but
  remember, we're all 97 per cent ape. If he does this,
  it's just his subconscious trying to make him look all
  powerful and manly and tell you that he likes you.
  Forgive the little chump and take it as a compliment.

If you see any of these signs, then, my clever friends, you've got your prey!

Get body language right and you can get any man. In the 1950s, researchers in behavioural psychology worked out that as much as 55 per cent of communication between humans is non-verbal. The actual words you use only count for about 7 per cent of the impact. (I found that out from one of my hours in the library – it's from Pease and Pease, *The Definitive Book of Body Language*.) So get your body to do the flirting and you're over halfway there.

Never reveal your little body language tricks to him, though. Don't tell him why you have men falling at your feet, or why you drove him mad with lust before you'd even exchanged a word. Men are ancient fools and need to believe the illusion that they were the predators who initiated contact. We both know that in fact he was the prey all along.

Eye contact + warm smile = eager attention

There are two more big flirting grounds I want to go through with you – the workspace and the Internet. Again, you can flirt like crazy and bag a man in each environment, but you have to be a bit more careful. Here are some tips.

Flirting at the office

A lot of relationships start in the workplace, but do be careful, my darlings. Romance in the office is *really* complicated.

The first thing to think about it is whether your crush is worth it. If you're too busy with work, you may perhaps only ever be meeting with people that you work with. You can develop crushes on people that are utterly unrealistic.

Let's give you an example. Me.

Gerry, 31

When I was on *Big Brother*. I was locked into a house, just seeing the same old people day in and day out. And I fell in love with a cameraman. Now, I didn't know much about this cameraman. I could only really see a silhouette of him through a two-way mirror near the bathroom, and the occasional glance when he hadn't put the blackout curtain back in place properly, but I had so little other stimulation that I decided I was in love with him. Or in love with his shadowy outline, anyway.

I never got anywhere. I didn't know his name. I didn't know if he was straight or gay. But I spent a lot of time flirting with a silhouette. (To be honest, I could have fallen in love with a shoebox if they'd put it in the house – I was that bored.)

This can happen in the office, too. If you don't go out enough fishing for new men, you can start falling for people in the office that you wouldn't ever consider in the outside world. Like the penniless postboy.

Now, girls, do watch out for this. The postboy is just for Christmas. (Or the night of the Christmas party!) Not for life.

Having said that, the office is a massive market, so why not have fun using it? You can practise flirting there every day and see what works. Use all the techniques in the book as you go about your daily office life. Use office situations to your advantage. Liven up dull meetings by playing with your body language as you sit opposite your prey. The dullest accounts strategy session can be seriously livened up with a strategically twitched ankle. Smile at that cute security guard. Do a bit of mirroring work on the boss.

Of course, if you do genuinely fall in love with someone in the office, there are all kinds of difficulties. For a start, your intended victim sees you every day, so you'll have to make an effort every day to look fabulous. Yes, I'm afraid you're going to have to always dress in high heels, stockings, make-up, all those little tricks to get your man! You'll never catch him if you rock up every day in a big old stained woolly sweater with lanky hair.

Another difficulty is secrecy. The biggest advice I can give you here is never, ever, *ever* confide anything to your colleagues. Don't tell them you fancy anyone. Don't tell them if you go out with anyone. Save all gossip for your friends outside the workplace.

Let's look at a case study to illustrate. My friend Rachel. Rachel (twenty-five) is one of the most gorgeous women I know – a striking mixed-race girl, with enormous 'manga comic' eyes, a perfect body and a sense of fashion. And the girl has brains! She works at a top-notch firm handling major corporate accounts and she's a social butterfly, Cosmo-drinking and finger-food eating at all the must-be-seen-at parties and clubs.

She should be having a fantastic love life, not ending up as a case study of examples to avoid in this book. So what did Rachel do wrong?

Well, she dated her employer, Thomas. Pay attention to this case study. It's long. But then she made a lot of mistakes.

Rachel and Thomas
Thomas was a rising force in the legal business with a very competitive package. Late thirties, gorgeous to look at, beautiful house, drove a Porsche, had high-powered friends, smoked Cohibas, wore Italian couture. When a woman looked at him the only thing she could think of was: 'Which private school would be the best for our perfect twin children?'

One Tuesday night Rachel was doing serious overtime for an acquisition and she was stuck in the office with Thomas and no dinner whatsoever. At around eleven when the job was done, she was packing her bag to go home when Thomas casually asked whether she had had anything to eat and, if not, whether she wanted to 'go grab a late bite'. As her other option was a grilled cheese sandwich and TV, she nonchalantly replied: 'Sure, why not.' They got in his car, drove to a nice restaurant, had dinner, complimented each other, played 'hand fondling under the table' and ended up snogging at three a.m.

On Wednesday, they went to the acquisition meeting. Afterwards they snogged a bit more. On Thursday they texted each other all day and locked themselves in Thomas's office for more snogging. On Friday they went out to the prearranged office party, got a bit tipsy and Thomas caressed her leg in front of everyone. Later on that night they finally slept together.

When Rachel woke up on Saturday morning in Thomas's place everything seemed perfect. He produced freshly washed Egyptian cotton towels and made her a breakfast of scrambled eggs, fresh fruit juice, coffee. They enjoyed music, a laugh and some more fabulous afternoon sex.

Around Saturday afternoon she decided to go back home and freshen up and meet up with her mates, while Thomas went off and played his usual round of Saturday tennis. They had an agreement to meet for Sunday lunch and early drinks. Before she started getting dressed, Thomas sat her down for the 'working together and sleeping together' talk, where he explained that it would not be wise for people to know as it would be a bit awkward and unprofessional, and that they should find the right time to let people know. Rachel half-heartedly agreed.

But she didn't stick to it. To Thomas's shock, she called her brother and asked him to pick her up from the house. She also then called her work colleagues and her parents and told them everything. To make things worse, she even sent a string of texts describing Thomas's performance and her infatuation with him. He found them when he peeked at her mobile on their next date (typical specimen of distrusting male).

The next afternoon, Thomas brought Rachel into his office. He explained that even though he really fancied her and thought she was great, he believed in mutual decisions and communication. He added that the whole story was a mistake and that they should not see each other any more.

Oh, Rachel! The boss! A Porsche! Egyptian cotton towels! Scrambled eggs (probably organic too)! How could you mess this one up!

Okay, this is a long story, but just about everything that could go wrong did go wrong for our heroine here. On paper, this girl had everything, but what she was lacking was confidence. There are women out there who are less successful at work, not as pretty, not as talented. But they have confidence in themselves and so they succeed. Rachel, however, was so delighted at her conquest, and so surprised at her luck, that she got everything wrong.

Of course the poor thing was infatuated with the man, but she should have played it mean. She should have played it down. She should have ignored him a bit and not 'advertised her success' by telling the whole world. She had only been with the man for five minutes, yet she was texting, ringing and boasting about him. She was even making calls whilst Thomas was still in the room, for goodness' sake.

Rachel should have been clever enough to gossip in secret. She should have deleted all the sent messages from her phone just in case the man decided to have a flick through. (Men *do* do this, girls, so bear this in mind when you're singing their praises by text.)

Rachel lost the man because she made *him* feel like the catch. Men who are good catches need to be brought down off their high horses and made to feel less important and needed, or you'll never get to keep them.

If I was Rachel I'd have done a bit of reverse psychology. Told him that I wanted to keep *him* secret. She should have said that she had no intention of getting a reputation as the office slut who was secretly bedding the boss. That would have made him feel less important and more like he was the one getting the catch.

Thomas asked her to stay in the firm as she was a valued employee, but Rachel has since ended up actually leaving the firm, because things got so awkward.

She lost her job, she lost Mr Porsche, and she lost face in the office – but let her losses be your lesson. Keep office romances a secret!

Flirting on the Internet

Some people think Internet dating is sad. There's a taboo about it. What nonsense!

Internet dating is taking over the market.

Newspaper lonely-heart advertising columns are so dated now. Who reads those any more? Who has time to send off letters? It's all happening on the web instead. It's fast, it's got photos, and it works. It also gives you an instant network of men to practise flirting with, including thousands who may not live in your city and who you'd never get to talk to otherwise.

I've had relationships with people who I've met on the Internet. And I know of several other people who have too. We live in the twenty-first century. You should try it! If you don't try it you're missing out on a massive, massive market.

And think of the advantages. If you have a desk job with a computer, and a boss who isn't around that much, you can actually use your company's time to look for a partner! I found several wonderful dates on the web when my poor bosses at Sotheby's thought I was hard at work. How fabulously practical. You can while away your days looking for love – and get paid for it! Now what on earth is sad about that?

There are dedicated Internet dating sites where you can advertise for potential partners (more about them in a bit), but first off, why not try flirting a little on sites like MySpace and Facebook?

These sites are called social networks – but really they're a massive database of people you can flirt with. You can look at people's sites, see if they're single. See what their friends look like. Say hello to their friends. It's great. And if you get your own social networking site, it'll be easy for potential new men to track you down.

Let's do a case study to demonstrate. Let's make it about me again.

Gerry, 31

I found one partner through Facebook. I'd met him at a conference, told him I was a specialist on Cycladic idols (Bronze Age, Aegan figurines). He got in touch via Facebook claiming he wanted this rare book on figurines.

Of course, later on, when we were in a relationship, he admitted that he'd had the book all along – in fact it was lying next to his computer. But the lesson here is that I'd been easy to track down via the Facebook site, and we could start a conversation and both use the excuse that it was simply about social networking. Of course it wasn't – like I said, these sites are really all about flirting! You can find all sorts of people on there.

www.myspace.com is the daddy of all, and nearly everyone I know is on it, but there's also fun to be had on the hugely popular *www.facebook.com*. They say it's a 'social utility that connects you with the people around you', but, again, all that electronic poking is just about flirting really.

www.ning.com is the latest gigantic trend where you can 'create, customise, and share your own social network for free', say the makers. But again, all this talk about customising social networks is really a big cover for single people tracking each other down and flirting around in cyberspace.

Internet dating sites

As well as all these sites you can gatecrash and use for flirting, there are several dedicated sites specifically for dating. They all require you to set up a profile, and, either for free or for a small monthly fee, offer access to the profiles of your potential partners.

Here are some examples:

- *www.Parship.co.uk* – you'll need some real boyfriend material to work with – and *Parship.co.uk* is the online dating service to supply it. The matching starts with a compatibility test, developed by psychologists who follow my hero, Sigmund Freud. Taking you beyond looks and shared interests, *Parship* recommends men with the right personality for you. It even offers free professional advice from

Dr Nafsika Thalassis, PhD (another Greek expert on getting your man!). There are hundreds of thousands of UK men on *Parship*, so at least one of them is bound to be right for you.

- *www.match.com* – a very successful dating site in the UK. Very easy to use interface.
- *www.datingdirect.com* – another big player in the dating market, launched with the slogan 'Same dating, new rules'. 3.5 million UK profiles to navigate for a small monthly fee.
- *www.metrodate.co.uk* – with message boards from all the major cities on which anyone can post.
- *www.perfectmatch.com*
- *www.loveandfriends.com*

The Internet also caters for particular communities and ethnic and religious groups. Below are some recommendations and some of the biggest names which my friends have used. This isn't a full list though – there are thousands out there.

- *www.jdate.com* and *www.jewishfriendfinder.com* for Jewish dates.
- *www.salaamlove.com* and *www.muslima.com* are two great dating sites for Muslims.
- Indian culture, even with its tradition of arranged marriages, is aided by *www.indiandating.com*.

- *www.bigchurch.com* for Christian dating.
- *www.deafsinglesconnection.com* for those with hearing impairment.

Message boards

You can also gatecrash message boards. Start chatting to people who enjoy and care about the same things you do. They may organise events or get-togethers – and you never know, it may lead to romance.

http://messages.yahoo.com and *http://groups.google.co.uk* are groups for discussion of topics from cinema to eastern philosophy, from design to travel to environment, and even how to grow an avocado tree! Sharing your social interests and hobbies may just lead to meeting the man of your dreams. What have you got to lose?

Whatever your little peccadillos, just search on the Internet – I'm sure you'll find a site out there that caters for you.

Your Internet profile

If you're going to go down the route of placing an Internet ad on a dating site, then take care with your Internet profile. Your profile is your advertising window. A recent photograph is essential – smile, please! It's perfectly okay if you cheat a little. Feel free to use Photoshop and beautify it – retouch spots, matt a shiny nose, take off a beer stain and crop the unwanted background. It's still you! Everyone does it. Liz Hurley airbrushes her bikini shots all the time. Don't go over the top, though. Cutting and pasting in somebody else's body is naughty!

Never choose a picture where you're with a bunch of friends on holiday. You don't want to have to give an explanation – 'I'm the fourth on the left with the straw hat next to the donkey' – and also you risk potential suitors thinking, 'Damn I wish she was the second babe on the right in the red bikini!'

Pick a photo where you look happy, tanned and fabulous. Every time you have a nice new picture taken, whack it up there! Countless men peruse dating sites on a daily basis. Their eyes get used to the same photos. A new picture of gorgeous you will attract their attention afresh.

As well as your picture, it's important to get your profile name right. Something like MissPartyTime sounds slutty. Instead, pick something that describes your physical appearance as well as your character in a positive light. For example: Funnygirl23, Dreambrunette36.

Your description has to be concise, positive and honest. But bear in mind that I said honest, not modest. Have you seen the competition out there? Just as with work CVs, everyone lies on the Internet. We all massage the facts a little. Those who claim that they haven't included any creatively crafted bullshit on their CV are either liars or still unemployed. So do the same for your dating CV in cyberspace.

It's fine to choose your most flattering picture. Fine to shave a few years off your age, a few millimetres off your thighs and maybe exaggerate how stunningly successful you are. But remember he has to meet you at some point, so don't overdo it. You may be able to get away with a photo that's five years out of date. One that's five stone out of date is harder to live up to!

Also remember that it goes both ways. That income may not be as high as he claims. He may not be as tall, as young, as thin or as successful as he says. Yes, I'm afraid you may have to brace yourself for disappointment, as Mr Wonderful may be telling a few porkies too.

Again, I'd advise you to approach your Internet dating like you would a job. Organise your selling points and add in key words, the same way you would with a CV. Keep improving the information whenever you have some inspiration. Ask friends for advice and for your best points. This is your online advertisement. You're selling yourself. Make it attractive.

Here are some common errors I want you to avoid:

- ✗ *Favourite pastimes: clubbing and pole dancing.* Are you serious? He'll never think, 'There is a girl to start a family with.'
- ✗ *Favourite food: pizza and chips.* That will not do! Try to be more sophisticated. Perhaps talk about an amazing dish that you can cook.
- ✗ *Favourite Film: Dirty Dancing.* Too common, too chick-flick! But Tarantino is great and considered

cult by men. Write *Kill Bill 1* and he'll visualise you as a hot action-chick!

✗ *Not supplying a photo.* No one will reply. Come on, you're not that ugly. Stick a pic in.

✗ *Not specifying what you're looking for.* What? You'll take anything, will you? Are you really that desperate?

✗ *Describing yourself as 'bubbly'.* Dreadful, overused, and many men have disclosed to me that it has connotations of the plump girl who binge-drinks at every party. (Translation = slut.) There are so many better ways to sell your enthusiastic personality.

✗ *I like curling up on the sofa with a nice a bottle of wine and a good DVD.* Terrible. I know you like that, but so do 80 per cent of the profiles I have viewed on match.com. I'm not going to tell you what to write because you'll all end up having identical profiles, but as an example, how about: *I'm as comfortable at a cocktail party in a strapless long dress as in jeans and T-shirt spending quality 'couch time'* which implies you're fun at parties and great in a more domestic environment as well. Notice the description of 'long dress' – it makes them visualise you as a stylish siren.

✗ *Spelling mistakes.* When you've completed your profile, check your spelling and show it to a friend. They'll also be able to pick up on anything discouraging in the description or ridiculous points you thought were highly amusing. Show it to a man, too – ask him what he thinks and if there's anything that would put him off.

How to flirt on the Internet

Okay, that's your ad sorted. Now let's learn how to track down the prey that's out there advertising in cyberspace.

Most sites offer the Quick Search option, so you can browse the twenty-first-century equivalent of a tribal display of males by their Internet profiles!

You can search by various different criteria – shared interests, age groups, areas, height, even financial status.

You will get hundreds of matches, so follow your instinct and narrow it down to about twenty to thirty people. Drop the bait to these lucky chosen few.

Even in cyberspace, the mean rules apply. It's way better if you allow men to come to you. But since you can't use your arsenal of body language signals, you send 'emoticons' instead. You know, these things – :) : (.

All you need to send is a simple email message with just a smiley face, and something like 'Hey', 'Nice' or 'Great profile'. Nothing more flattering. The ones that like your profile photograph will soon reply.

A vixen like you will receive heaps of emails in response to your profile. Read them all, but be exceedingly picky so you don't waste time. Only answer one in five or so, and skim their replies again.

Your reply should be a generic email (fine-tune it as time goes by) that you copy and paste and send to each man, with the addition of a few phrases commenting on something you've read in his profile. 'I can't believe you also love this movie!' Keep correspondence going with a maximum of five to six males and check your computer each evening to see who's been responding. (Of course, if you're lucky enough to have an office computer and a boss who doesn't check on you much, you may be able to log in during the day for a quick work-break flirt!)

A good trick for juggling more than one Internet romance at once is to open a few Word documents, title each one with the username of a man of interest and from then onwards copy and paste their messages and your replies. This way you can keep track of your replies. It's fine to send the same reply to more than one – it will let you compare and contrast how they respond. When you email them back, ask questions so they feel the necessity to reply and you get into an email conversation with them.

These techniques work. Think of that skilful ex-boyfriend of mine that wanted the advice on the art book. I was so convinced of his love for books on figurines that I offered to give him a private gallery tour. (Which turned into a drinks date and a relationship.) After a few weeks of email flirting move to a phone conversation, followed by the first short and introductory coffee date. (I'll tell you how to handle that little event on page 127.)

Now, a word of warning. The Internet is a great place to practise flirting, but again, you must follow the rules.

Don't start revealing all to the man, talking about your childhood, your job, your hopes, your fears. All online. All before you've even met. I've seen girls have these fabulously long Internet conversations and believe they've found a soulmate, then wonder why he disappears. Or they get to a date and it's a disaster. Of course it's going to go wrong. When he meets you it'll all be an anticlimax because he'll already know everything about you. You'll end up repeating everything he's read about you already.

Another word of warning.

Watch out for dirty old men.

Not surprisingly, due to its anonymity, cyberspace is chock-a-block with perverts and old men. (Nurse, he's out of the bed and web-surfing again.) Think basic safety, girls. *Never give out your home address, home telephone number or work number. Don't tell him exactly where you work.* The Internet is full of stalkers. And liars. Until you know that he's genuine, give him a mobile number only. If you're emailing him, check your email address doesn't give your company's name. Maybe set up an email address that you use just for Internet flirting.

When you meet up, meet in a public place, and, again, *do not provide him with your home address or personal details.* And never sleep with anyone for three months after meeting them. (Yes, I know that rule may come as a shock – there's more about it on page 137.) The three-month delay will discourage people who are just trawling around for sex.

The beauty of the Internet is that once you're in a relationship, you can still use the web to keep him on his toes.

On all sites it's relatively straightforward to freeze your account. Don't do that. He'll perceive that as a weakness – you're saying you want to be just with him, and he'll get comfy. Keep your profile online (you put so much genius and effort into composing it that it's a shame not to). Check it from time to time. He'll be able to see that you're checking it (online profiles have a 'last viewed' feature). It will keep him alert and on his best behaviour.

Only ever shut down your account if either the relationship gets genuinely serious or he asks you for exclusivity for himself (which is not an easy thing for a man to ask, so he really likes you). Then it's only fair.

Oh, look at me. Jumping forward to serious commitment and exclusivity already! First I'd better talk you through how to turn all these gorgeous little flirtatious meetings and messages into a date.

Let me be honest with you. If the man likes you, he'll ask for a date. If he doesn't ask, it's more than likely that he's not interested. Sorry.

There are a couple of things you can try to give it one last push, but if neither of these works, then give up and move on whilst your dignity is intact.

1. Ask him out face to face

If you've dropped the bait, done the flirting with your eyes and your body language, and you feel there's chemistry there but he still hasn't asked for your number, you may have to be more proactive. There's a book from America called *The Rules* that says you should never approach a man you're interested in. But maybe that doesn't work for British men. Sometimes they need a bit of a push.

I don't really recommend this as it goes against all the mammoth-hunting rules. There could be reasons why he hasn't asked you. He may not be single, for example. But there's no harm in finding out for sure, so I can allow you to take the first step into making the date. Just a small step, mind. A little tiny subtle geisha step. Say, 'I don't usually do this, but here's my number if you ever need to know about [insert some excuse here like Cycladic art].' Or mention that you're on Facebook.

Notice that this is subtle. Remember you're a mammoth. Not a slut. He has to think it's his idea. But just occasionally, it doesn't hurt to make the first move. Be bold. Ask him. Always carry cards with your number on.

If you see a stranger on a train or platform you can perhaps be even more upfront. Try the line: 'I'm used to being pursued, but you're very special. Here's my number and email.' He's a stranger. You may never see him again. What have you got to lose? I should have done that last week with a gorgeous man I passed by in the street. I've been thinking about him ever since and wish I'd been a bit bolder now.

Try these extreme techniques, wait and watch your inbox and hope he takes the bait. If he likes you enough, he'll call. If not, just move on without a backward glance. You've dangled the bait, given the clues. If he's still too scared to ring you, forget him. He clearly has no balls. Why would you want to be with a man who has no balls? You should always keep your sights on the better man.

2. Ask him out by phone/Internet

What if you've swapped numbers, there was definite chemistry between you, but he doesn't call?

Leave it for three days. Hopefully he'll have called/ texted by then, but if not then perhaps you can make one geisha step in his direction. A tentative call/text/ Facebook poke would perhaps be in order. Compose it carefully, avoid ambiguities and leave multiple avenues open for him to come back on, for example, 'Hi, its Esmeralda here, very much enjoyed meeting you on Saturday, perhaps we could meet up soon and carry on the conversation.' Reasonably light, forthright without being suffocating, but unignorable. Don't use abbreviations – you'll look like a silly teenager. Spell it all out.

Only do this once, however. And take the hint if there's no response. This is all the man-chasing that I'll allow. Remember, we have to make him think he's the hunter.

Drop him that hint, and if he doesn't call, doesn't pursue, then move on to the next.

If he calls – the rules of the telephone

If the man asks you out, it's all so much easier. He's hooked. He wants you. So enjoy playing a few games as you reel him in.

The rise of the mobile phone has caused a whole catalogue of problems for girls. It can make you seem all too available. Remember, just because he can call you any time, anywhere, it doesn't mean you have to answer.

At the start of every dating adventure, you must be disciplined. This is a very emotional time and the temptation will be to start pinning hopes on this new man. Restrain yourself! Don't start embroidering monogrammed his and hers pillows yet! Or planning the wedding frock. Take deep breaths and try to be as relaxed as possible and realise that you're in control of the situation. You have to act like you don't care that much and are used to being chased by adoring men all the time.

Don't worry, it's easy to fake. Follow these rules:

Don't agree to a date straight away
First of all, you mustn't be available for a date too easily. He needs to pursue you. If he calls you to arrange a date, give a positive reaction and be very sweet on the phone but don't agree to meet him straight away on the first date he suggests. Always make him wait whilst you ask if you can 'check your diary' and ring him back. Don't ring back for hours. A day is even better. That will guarantee he's spending his day thinking about you and hoping you go on the date. The whole idea is that you appear as a catch, the girl that everybody wants. He has to wait to see if he's lucky enough to get a date with you.

Don't offer an explanation why you can't make the date. If he demands to know why you can't go out on a certain night just tell him one of these:

- You're moving house.
- You're going to see such a boring play that you are too embarrassed to tell him the name of it. (Okay, you're really going for a manicure, highlights and full-on waxing session to get ready for the date with him, but he needn't know that.)
- You haven't read the last two editions of *Vanity Fair* yet.
- Nothing must interfere with your little poker club.

Just have confidence and try it. It works. Trust me.

Here's a case study:

Amy, 33

Amy told her new boyfriend over a series of weeks that she was moving house and couldn't date him at that time. Now her husband, he still jokes about it today. And of course she's still too busy to do the mundane things in life as she is always moving house.

Of course you'll agree to see him eventually. You're just giving him a little delay to make him sweat (and give you time for a facial).

Never reply to texts too quickly

Never reply to texts straight away. It's much better to make them wait for it. Think of a game of poker. If you win at cards within the first five minutes, then the game is no fun at all. But if you've spent a whole night playing it, chasing the goal, and then you win, you feel a real sense of pleasure. So put your poker hat on when it comes to texting.

Never answer in under an hour. Ever. Leave it two hours if possible. Again, a day is better if you can bear it. It gives the impression you're massively busy, possibly fighting off lots of other men, even if all you're really doing is watching the *EastEnders* omnibus in your pyjamas.

I know it's very tempting to text back straight away, because you're excited. *But don't.* You'll probably notice that if you leave it two hours, he'll answer your text straight away. This is an excellent sign. It means you have him dangling.

I call it the Joan Collins technique. Think of yourself as Ms Collins in *Dynasty*. Actually, she can be my next case study.

Alexis
Dex Dexter texts Alexis for a date. But Alexis is running Colby Co Oil Empire. She's in mid-negotiation with the Arabs on the oil deal. She's got three princes waiting to see her. She's due a catfight with Krystle. And she's got to choose some diamonds and some new shoulder pads in a minute because her stylist is downstairs.

Now, she wouldn't text Dex back immediately, would she? No. She'd leave it at least three hours. (And her name at one point was Alexis Morrell Carrington Colby Dexter Rowan, which should give you a clue about how successful she was with men.) Every time you get a text, think Alexis and wait a while. It'll drive him crazy.

Never ring him
Apart from that first, tiny step of a call to give the man a nudge when he needs it, you should never, ever chase a

man by phone. If you've been on a date, no matter how good, wait for the man to call you. It's a game of strength. It's about who's going to crack first. And, girls, we're not going to crack first. Even if it's been two weeks, we're not going to crack. Actually, if it's been two weeks, then it's never going to work. He's not interested. He's busy with another date. Get over him.

Sorry to be so harsh, but that's real life. If the man wants you, he'll chase you. If he doesn't chase, then you have no future. If you do the chasing, you may get him on a temporary basis. You may spend weeks, months, years using all your tricks to lure him in, but it will never work because he didn't ever get the thrill of the chase.

It may hurt at the time, but the best thing to do is let the man go if he clearly isn't into you and isn't chasing you. Forget about him. It will save time in the long term. It may seem that you are letting opportunities for romance go, but you're not. You're protecting yourself.

Enough of the doom. You're a fabulous woman. That little sucker might not have phoned. But another one will. And when he does …

Keep it short

Again, we follow the rules on phoning and texting and let him chase. Let him phone you. When you phone the man back, keep the conversation short. Just tell him what day you're available so he can take you out. Don't launch into the details of everything you've been doing at work that day, or where you're going now, or you did with the girls over the weekend, or how your top-lip-wax hurt. You want an air of mystique. You want him to worry a little bit about what you've been up to, where you've been. With whom.

Do all this, my little mammoths, and our hunter will think he'd better get cracking and get a date with fabulous, busy, gorgeous little you in the diary before another caveman gets in there with his club.

PART THREE

How to Treat Him Mean When You're Dating Him

'Girls are like pianos.
When they're not upright, they're grand.'
BENNY HILL

Girls, I insist you remain vertical throughout this chapter.
GERRY

The first three dates

There are certain rules you must play by for the first three dates with a man. You need to be in control of the whole dating process from day one, but to lull the man into an entirely false sense that *he* is in control.

Remember, there is still everything to play for. Nothing is in the bag. He's probably seeing lots of other girls too at this stage. You're hopefully seeing lots of other men too. But here's how to get through those first three meetings and leave him convinced that you're the only girl for him.

The first date
The first date should be in a coffee shop. It isn't really a date at all. It's a preview. It's an audition to see if you really want to invest a whole date in this man.

Dress alluringly, but carefully. Decide what's provocative and sexy without being cheap and sluttish. (For more tips on what to wear, see page 33.)

The History Channel technique

You need to keep this first date very short. Forty-five minutes. One hour maximum. Trust me. Even if it's going brilliantly you *must* leave early.

Think of yourself as being one of those preview ads on the History Channel. They pop up for twenty seconds, promising they'll tell you all sorts of fantastic things in a new programme. They tease you. And then you tune in to watch the programme and find out the dirty details. Follow their example. Hint and tease about what's to come. Then leave. He'll love the preview and he'll want to tune in for the date.

The Churchill dog technique

Like I said, the trick is not to talk, it's to listen. The art of being a good conversationalist is actually to be a good listener. If you're not a good listener, then don't worry. You can just fake it with body language. Have you ever seen those Churchill insurance ads with the dog? The one that nods all the time? Do that. Be that dog. As he blathers on about his work and himself and some childhood holiday in a caravan, just nod. The trick is to do it in sets of three – nod, nod, nod. Just like the dog. Yes, yes, yes. You don't even really need to be listening to him when you do this – you could be thinking about the H&M sale – but just look in his direction. Pause, and then nod again a few seconds later. He'll think you're hanging on his every word. He'll think you're fabulous. You can use this technique in a relationship for decades. It works for bosses too.

If you use these two techniques, it'll all go well. After his forty-five minutes are up, he'll go back to his office and tell everyone that he's met the most *fantastic* woman who *really* understands him and he can't wait to meet her again. You can then go off to H&M.

Think of this date as an audition to see if you want to be lovers. Of course you'll get through his audition using these rules, but actually, secretly, this is all an audition for *him*. Do *you* want to see *him* again? Check him over during the date. He may not be perfect. He may not be as tall or as handsome as you'd like. But does he have other things going for him? Look for a guy with potential. If he's not that good-looking but he's charismatic and successful, then give him a chance even if he's not your usual type. Keep your mind open. You'll never get absolutely everything you want in a man. Be prepared to let some things go. No one's perfect. Even Brad Pitt has acne scars.

For you naughty little gold-diggers out there who are looking for a man of means to keep you in Jimmy Choos, if his earnings are low, try and work out if he's ambitious enough for a potential change of career, promotion or pay rise. Hardly any ladies marry men who are already rich, but you can easily marry a guy who's going to be rich. Roman Abramovich, Britain's second richest man (according to *The Times* Rich List 2006), met ex-wife Irina during a flight while he was a small-time businessman and she was an Aeroflot stewardess. The dashing blonde saw potential in the man. Okay, they ended up divorcing but she got a £155m divorce settlement. That must have eased her pain.

If you're looking for an Abramovich of your own, be prepared to overlook a few flaws – like him being really ugly. Remember, even the ugliest men look really handsome if they're covered in banknotes. (Look, don't start being shocked by all this advice – you're the one who's going out there looking for a man to bankroll you. I'm just pointing out that the first thing that attracts you to your multimillionaire future husband may not be his looks.)

A few little Internet investigations may be in order after this first date. MySpace him. Facebook him. Track down everything you can on him on the Internet. Facebook will also give you some nice little clues about whether there are other women in his life. Newspaper sites should tell you whether he's ever done anything that's ended up in the papers, good or bad.

Go back to your little black book after the date and fill in a little checklist.

- Did he have nice manners? Did he pull the chair out for you to be seated? Tell you that you looked good? Was he nice to the waiters? Did he get there on time?

- Did he have good taste in clothes? (No gold jewellery, I hope. Medallions are an instant dumping offence.)
- Did he have a good sense of humour? Remember, these will have been his best 'first date' jokes. It'll go downhill from here. If he can't make you laugh, then run away now. It'll be a dull life. It's too late for him; save yourself.
- Did he have bad breath or BO? First date is as fragrant as he's going to get, so if it's bad at this stage, bail out now.
- What about his table manners? Can you bear to sit opposite that for the next twenty years?
- Did he answer his phone or check his BlackBerry while he was with you? Unless he's a doctor on call with lots of lives to save, he should really be able to give you his undivided attention for forty-five minutes.
- Was he well-groomed, with recently trimmed hair, no odd mole sproutings and clean fingernails? Were his shoes polished?
- Did you check the ring finger of his left hand for traces of a white, untanned line?
- Did he look after you – hail a cab for you after the date, for example? Or offer you a lift?
- And finally (every girl should have a little element

of the gold-digger about her at this stage – there's no harm in checking him out for signs of money) was his wallet leather? Were the cards inside platinum? Did he have a decent watch? Was he driving a decent car, or did he arrive on a skateboard? I'm not saying you should only go for a man with cash, but there's nothing wrong with wanting stability, security and a very nice house. (Keep in mind how impossibly expensive children are since the invention of game consoles and MP3 players.)

- Talking of which, did he pay? Come on! It was only coffee! If he's going Dutch at this stage when it's only two lattes, then he's a touch on the stingy side.

Now remember, be ruthless at this stage. If there was nothing happening in the chemistry department, bin him. Fill the slot with someone else. If he was rude or looked like a player, also dump him. You haven't got time to date cr*p men.

Even if there's been *great* chemistry. Do *not* kiss him on this date. It's only been a coffee, you hussy.

The second date
This can be either lunch, or an early evening drink.

Let him be the one to suggest where to meet. That way you'll see if he knows where to go and if he's willing to take you somewhere nice. Be fussy and don't agree to just a drink at the pub. Darling, you simply don't do pubs (you do chic cocktail bars and eateries). Also let him know that you would prefer a lunch date to dinner. (You should never go out with a guy at night when you don't know him that well.)

If it's lunch, he knows there's going to be no sex, so you're giving him a sign that he's going to have to work to pursue you. If he's gentleman enough to invest time in you, and he's not just after a legover, he'll have lunch. If he doesn't 'do' lunch, then basically he can p*ss off to some tramp.

Date two will be slightly longer than the first date. You should still think 'preview' and not reveal too much of yourself. Don't blurt out your life story. Why would he meet you again if you have nothing more to say?

Don't talk about your problems. Yes, of course, further down the line men are looking for someone to share problems, low moments and dramas with, but he's not looking for it on the second date.

Remember that on these early dates you're giving him an idealised version of you. This is not cheating, it's just playing smart. He'll find out the real stuff later on. But by then, he'll be attached and he'll be in love.

Again, no kissing. Make him wait. You should be aiming to pique his interest and leave him yearning for more. The trick is to unfold gradually like a beautiful flower. Don't hand yourself over on a plate like a suckling pig!

The third date

The third date is the crucial dinner date. The good news is that you can also kiss him on this date, so it's a fun one.

This date is the most important after the short, early 'qualifying' ones. A dinner date shows you like someone. You're investing a whole evening in him and him alone. You're letting him get somewhere. He's a very lucky man.

Take him to a restaurant that you're reasonably familiar with as this will boost your confidence. You wouldn't arrange a vital business meeting in territory you haven't tested in advance, would you? Use your body language skills: focus on him. No wandering eyes, please, no matter how cute the waiters are. Avoid noisy restaurants; raising your voice just to be heard is unflattering. Candlelit ones are good. Candles on tables will take off about five years and six pounds.

Eat your food, but not everything! All good heterosexual men get turned on by women eating. It's a basic instinct. But always have great manners. Men get very turned on by women with good manners, and this includes eating. Every woman should watch herself eat in front of a mirror. If you enjoy the food and he asks, tell him. Men make a strong connection between sex and food. If you don't enjoy it, tell him why as well, but always phrase things in a nice way.

Now – and this might make me unpopular with some of you – the big no-no here is alcohol.

Let me explain with another case study. Let's call her

Miss Prada Shoes

The other day I was in London, near Liverpool Street Station. It was a Friday night and all these City people were going home after a night's drinking. I saw this woman. Late thirties. I could tell from the way she was dressed that she was a real high-flyer. Probably been promoted several times. She had this gorgeous Escada suit on. Her hair was straight from an expensive salon. She had Prada shoes.

But she was drunk. Very drunk. I wasn't quite near enough to see, but I think there was vomit in her expensively highlighted hair. Her colleagues were with her, begging taxis to stop and take her. Eventually one did. I watched as she stumbled in, then as her colleagues threw in her handbag after her. And those Prada shoes, which had been left on the pavement.

Now, when Miss Prada Shoes arrived at work the next Monday morning, her colleagues would no longer see her as the boss in the Escada suit. They'd seen her lose control. She might have worked for fifteen years to earn their respect – fifteen years of waking up at six o'clock and late nights at the office, and it was all gone in one night. They'd seen her off her face.

Okay, back to you. It's the same with a relationship. You could put in weeks, months, years of seduction, but if he sees you staggering about like Miss Prada Shoes, you'll have lost it all. You will lose him.

Never, *ever* get drunk on these early, crucial dates. If you want to go out and get hammered, then do it with your friends. Go away for the weekend for an alcoholiday. It's fine for your friends to see you like that. They'll forgive you and still love you and you'll all have fun. He won't think it's so funny. He should only ever see you accessorised with a handbag. Not vomit in your hair.

I found a paper by Sir Walter Raleigh the other day in the library. In it he warned that wine 'transformeth a Man into a Beast, decayeth Health ... deformeth the Face and rotteth the Teeth.' That was written four hundred years ago – but the advice still stands – booze will still rotteth your twenty-first-century teeth, girls.

Personally, I don't think you should *ever* let a man see you drunk, never mind just in the early stages, but even when you're firmly a couple. I think you lose your mystique. It's just not a good look.

Many great dates have failed at this obstacle. I dated a gorgeous man in the past, but I dumped him because of alcohol. He wasn't an alcoholic, but he'd regularly have one too many. And lose control. Or, if he wasn't with me, he'd start ringing me and slurring stupid things down the line. It wasn't cute, it was annoying.

The art of being mean, of seducing your man, is all

about retaining control. If you're drunk, you won't be in control. My lovely late grandmama Anastasia used to remark, 'The spirit is willing but the flesh is weak,' and that's especially true after a couple of glasses of spirits. Stay strong and stay in control.

To avoid temptation, it may be a good idea to drive to these crucial dates, then you can't go over the limit. If you must drink, then for goodness' sake make sure you don't drink more than him. Watching you hoover up a bottle of wine is *not* attractive.

Sorry, but there's another big no-no here. And it's sex.

The three-month rule

'Give a man a free hand and he'll run it all over you.'
MAE WEST

Tell those little cavemen to keep those hands to themselves.
GERRY

If you read *Debrett's*, it says it's okay to sleep with the man on the third date.

No it's not.

Don't listen to *Debrett's*. It was written for posh girls, but look at how dysfunctional the upper classes all are. All the men have mistresses and all the women are really mixed-up. Maybe it's because they all read *Debrett's*.

If you have a castle or a sizeable trust fund, you may

be able to get away with some hussy-like behaviour. I've found that when a woman is worth millions or daddy owns a country, it automatically means that men are keener on you and tend to call for another date.

Debrett's may be written for ladies, but sleeping with a man on the third date is not the act of a lady. It's the act of a harlot. The good news is that you don't have to behave like a nun. I've said I will allow a kiss on date three, girls – after all, it's good to test the chemistry – but that's as far as it can go.

Most men divide women into two large categories – the ones they just want to have sex with, and the ones they would like to stick around for longer. All men want a taste of the forbidden fruit, but none lust after old melons that have been prodded by everyone else.

A prime directive in men's minds is to get the best and conquer it. Remain unconquered for a while – it will help get him well and truly hooked and convinced that you're the best.

So forget what *Debrett's* says. The only thing that is allowed to come off during dates one, two and three is your pashmina. The secret of seduction is to remain elusive. Not loose.

So how long do you remain elusive for? There's a book out there called *Not Tonight, Mr Right*, which says you should wait at least six months before sleeping with a man. Now, I think this *is* too long. No matter how bewitching you are, very few men will wait half a year for you to show him your duvet. But making him wait *three months* is a perfect timescale. It sounds like a long time, but it's crucial to wait this long because it's the only way of taming men's biology. Remember how we talked about how men are naughty little bullocks (page 26) and love hunting mammoth-types? The man will not enjoy the chase if you give in too soon. The longer the hunt, the more memorable the experience and the more valuable the catch.

So be prudish. By this, I don't mean be a vinegar-faced matron. I mean tease him, keep him interested, have lovely dates with him, kiss him, but keep your clothing on for a while. Trust me, men simply do not stay with 'easy' women. Yes, they have sex with them, maybe even a couple of times, but I'm afraid they don't view them as long term-prospects. I know it's sexist, it's outdated and it's unfair, and it's also something they'd never admit to a woman, but this is what my male friends tell me. As one friend put it after one night with a new 'lady', 'She slept with me so quickly; therefore, does she sleep with anyone with a postcode?', whereas another friend who had been made to wait a while turned up one day smiling like a cat that had finally caught a canary after a complicated chase around the house.

If you only want a one-night-stand, then go ahead. Hop into bed straight away. But if you want a man for the long haul then teach him that he's going to have to fight to get you. You're not a fait accompli, by any stretch! You're not easy. This is one canary who's going to put up a fight!

How to put him off without turning him off

- If, in the restaurant he says, 'Your place or mine?' smile cutely and tell him 'both'. You're going to yours and he's going to his. Then tap him on the knee and tell him he's naughty.
- If his hand heads south during a kiss, slap it away. Tut at him, then kiss him again.
- If you share a cab home, ask the driver to wait outside whilst he walks you to your door. Kiss him on the doorstep. He'll get all worked up because the meter on the cab is running whilst he kisses you. Good. He'll be hoping he'll be allowed to go back out and send the cab home without him, but you must not let him. Thank him nicely for dinner, then tell him 'no'.
- If he persists, don't say you have to 'get up early for a meeting'. That's so banal. Instead tell him 'no' in a cute way. Maybe say you have to go and feed your goldfish now. He knows you're taking the mickey, but he'll get the message. If he persists, try telling him the goldfish has to go to the vet in the morning as you're worried it's been a bit depressed recently. And you don't want to give it the stress of meeting strangers.

- If he's still hanging in there like a pit bull on heat, determined to get a 'cup of tea' tell him categorically: 'There will be other nights! Good night and thank you!' Wave and shut the door.

Trust me, the man will enjoy the chase. If he doesn't call you back after this, then it was all doomed anyway, but who cares – it was only a dinner date. Move on to the next man. If, however, you slept with him at this early stage and he didn't call, then you'd feel dreadful. The Three-Month Rule is all about self-respect and self-protection.

It will encourage the real men – the ones who genuinely want to be your partner. And it will discourage the so-called 'pick-up artists' who use dating as an excuse to sleep with as many girls as possible and have no interest in you and your life other than for sex.

There's another advantage to waiting, too. If you go dating around, but not sleeping around, you can see a lot more men. If you're not sleeping with them, nobody can accuse you of being a slut if you date more than one man at the same time, can they? Go on! Have lots of nights out with men who are lusting after you. Enjoy the company of a portfolio of men, all with their individual potential and possibilities. Let them all fight for you. And if any of them turn out to be losers, the disappointment will be lessened by the fact there are more suitors waiting. This technique has been used by women for millions of years. Helen of Troy had so many suitors they were able to form them all into an army to fight the Trojan war.

Here's a case study to illustrate the benefits of waiting:

Mike, 37

I started seeing two women at approximately the same time. I know it was cheeky, but I never promised exclusive rights to either. Danny was an actress and Kate was a primary school teacher. Physically I liked both. Danny had an amazing body, sculpted after years of stage school and dance practice. Kate was more voluptuous but her breasts were to die for. I slept with Danny from day one, after meeting her at an R&B night – the sex was great and she was always willing. But Kate just wasn't up for it. It was only after several dates that I managed to squeeze a decent snog out of her.

I became infatuated with Kate, fantasising holding her in my arms, undressing her, wondering what she would look like naked. I called her every day. I knew she liked me, but she was busy with her life and didn't always have time for me. Around the same time I realised I had no interest in Danny beyond the sex, and I finished it. She objected, but I explained to her that there was no real chemistry between us. I knew what I wanted and that was winning Kate. And it was the right choice. After two years together I have found my soulmate and I consider myself very, very lucky.

This point is also perfectly illustrated in *Sex and the City*.

Carrie Bradshaw and Aidan
Aidan, the hunky carpenter, ended up dating Carrie Bradshaw for two series of *Sex and the City*, after telling her in the early stages that he wanted to wait, for all the right reasons. As he said in one episode, he was fed up of bedding women too quickly and all the relationships then failing. He was fed up with being single. He wanted to sleep with someone that he cared about instead.

(Series Three, Episode Six, if you want to watch the exact scene!)

Of course, there are exceptions to the rule. There are people who sleep together at the very beginning. They get married. They have a happy family. But do you want to risk it? That's the question.

The only possible exception I might be prepared to make to this three-month 'waiting' rule is if he presents you with a diamond ring and proposes. (But even then I'd make him wait another twenty-four hours whilst you get it valued and make absolutely sure it's a decent rock. Not just something he picked up from the Argos sale.)

So that's the first three dates sorted. If you like him, carry on seeing him. Have fun and enjoy it. (Feel free to see other men too, of course.)

Here's a suggested dating schedule:

- 1st date – a coffee shop. One latte and you're out of there. Let him pay.
- 2nd date – lunch in a mid-price restaurant or an early-evening drink in a nice bar. Let him pay.
- 3rd date – dinner. Take him to a restaurant that you're reasonably familiar with. Offer to go Dutch on the bill, but don't try too hard. If he really is the one for you, he has to be gallant. Kiss him if you feel like it.
- 4th, 5th and 6th date – something fun that you'll enjoy. The zoo, an aquarium, the park, a museum, a sporting activity.
- 7th and 8th date – try the cinema and the theatre. A good film or play so you have something to discuss later, but nothing heavy. Forcing him to spend the night discussing Rainer Werner Fassbinder's *Die bitteren Tränen der Petra von Kant* when he really wanted to watch the completely meaningless summer action blockbuster could kill things at this stage.
- 9th and 10th dates – after this you can progress to a dinner at his – or yours – for future dates. But leave or kick him out afterwards. Remember, you do not share a duvet at this stage.

If you're just not in the mood, there's no point dragging yourself out to a date. Cancel the engagement but offer to reschedule. Remember, you're in control. He can only see you when you're feeling sensational.

We've covered where to go. Now, even more importantly what should you wear, and, when you're not nodding along pretending to be listening to him, what should you say?

What to wear
It's a good idea to have a series of outfits ready. A first-date outfit, a specific second-date outfit, and so on. This helps if you're juggling more than one man, and stops you worrying over whether he has already seen you in that particular dress. It will also save you cash. There's no need to buy a brand new outfit for every date. In fact you're better off in a tried-and-tested outfit that you know makes you look fabulous. You can always accessorise with new jewellery if you want to feel special. An unusual brooch or necklace is a good talking point, and of course strategically placed jewellery gives him a good excuse to take long, lingering, admiring looks at your bosom. Be careful, though – don't overaccessorise. I don't want you going out in full-on feathers like a Brazilian carnival float.

A suggestion of fabulous underwear is always good – perhaps some stockings under a long fitted pencil skirt. That will allow him to see a hint of a bump of a suspender belt through the material – but the skirt won't be so short that he can see your stocking tops when you sit down. Men love stockings. They have ready-for-action connotations, and the sound of expensive nylon rubbing alerts them like hounds. Think sexy, cheeky – but not cheap. Reveal a little of the legs or a little of the cleavage. If you've got a miniskirt on, wear a top that doesn't reveal too much. If your blouse is fitted, perhaps wear jeans. Never reveal too much. You're not on Page 3, and you're not Sharon Stone in *Basic Instinct*.

If it's cold, wear a coat. (Yes, your mother was right.) There's nothing less attractive than a girl who's turning blue in the street as she waits for a cab in her flimsy outfit. I see all these girls outside clubs in miniskirts, huddled and turning into ice, looking like those mummified corpses they find preserved in the Alps. It's not a good look. Wear a nice coat and take it to the cloakroom.

No G-strings. Oh, they look so cheap, especially when they're poking out over the top of your jeans. He should never see your underwear on a date. And do check what happens with your trousers when you sit down. Breast cleavage can be sexy. Bottom cleavage is most definitely not.

On the topic of underwear, if it's stuff that he can't see, feel free to cheat at this stage. Big hold-it-all-in Spanx Pants. Cast-iron corsets. Chicken fillets down underwired bras. He won't be getting to see any of this so you may as well wear everything you can that lifts, separates, holds in, pushes up and helps you pretend that you're an hour-glass beauty. When you dress, think of yourself as Gustav Eiffel designing the Eiffel Tower. A little bit of clever structural engineering and ironwork to make an impossible shape is entirely acceptable at this stage. By the time he realises that your flat tummy is encased in acres of industrial-strength knicker elastic, and your DD cup is made of rubber fillets and was bought from a department store the day before, he'll be in love and won't care.

What to say
Keep chatter about your personal life to a minimum. It will make you terribly mysterious and exciting. If you reveal every single detail of your childhood, studies, job, aspirations blah blah blah, what is there to hang around for? He'll find all this mystery refreshing after his previous date with the entomologist who burned his cerebral cortex with her vivid description of the breeding behaviour of coleopterans. Yes, I know you're excited, but you need to corset those emotions. Restrain yourself.

Let him do most of the talking. Ask open-ended questions – ones that can't be answered with a yes or no

– 'Where did you go on holiday this summer?' is a standard. Also try music, pets or sports activities. Have a glance at a newspaper or the TV news before you set off so you know roughly what's going on in the world that day. Forget the crap about not talking about religion or politics. These are the very things you judge a man upon. Can you talk a little about topics like immigrants, or will you sit there blankly? Turn the cards around, ask him about something that he's unlikely to be able to answer easily. If he complains about the government, ask him what he would do about it. Ask him if he voted. How people deal with their lack of knowledge is very telling. Is he someone who wants to find out more?

Having said that, whilst it's good to have an opinion, you shouldn't whine, bombard him with a speech or start shouting at him like you're Jeremy Paxman. And don't start moaning. Men hate moaning women. I've known some men who've come back from a first date and said they were considering emigrating, just to make sure they never saw the moaning, whining old bore again!

Talking about his childhood is also a good one. My late grandfather, who was a prominent psychiatrist in Greece, believed that the human personality is 'constructed' completely by the time we're three. He also claimed that the majority of our fears, traumas and complexes all originate back to childhood. You can find out a lot about the man by asking what he was like as a boy. Ask him pleasantly about his happiest childhood memories. If he starts narrating stories about fond summer holidays, school trips, pets etc., the chances are that he is a more or less balanced person. Heartfelt love for his parents, brothers and sisters is also a great indicator of a generous, loving nature.

When he asks you the same questions about holidays and childhood, try and give answers that engage all the senses. It's called the 'Positive Associations Technique', and it makes the man think that life will be fabulous with you. Talk to him about an amazing holiday you've been on. The heat, the warmth, the fabulous food. Talk about colours, tastes, light. The more vividly you describe it, the more vividly the picture will build in his mind. Does he like animals? Describe an adorable puppy you had as a child. Food? Mention a fabulous restaurant you visited. Or a dish you can make. Tempt him. You're saying, 'By being with me this is how life will be.' Pique his interest with sensuality and promises.

I use this technique all the time. If it's a grey winter's day, I talk about Greece. I might show them a book about Greece – gorgeous pictures of sun-washed white houses with views of a blue bay. Then I build on the initial stimulus by providing details that help him – the smell, the light, the easy life, the intensity of the fruits that ripen in the Mediterranean sun, the perfume of the wild herbs that permeates the atmosphere.

Come up with lots of bullshit like that and he'll leave the date all dreamy and thinking of hot sun and fabulous banquets in paradise. It works. They fall for it.

Give him a break if he says something stupid. Remember that's he's probably nervous about dating too. Just laugh it off. And upon greeting, don't hesitate to spoil him with compliments: 'I love your jacket/shirt', 'You smell great!' That will make him relax and think you're wonderful from the second he meets you.

Laugh and smile. The chances are that he's going to enjoy laughing with you as much as anything else. A spontaneous sense of humour is one of the most powerful aphrodisiacs for you both.

Do not – ever – talk about your sex life. He doesn't need to know. If you're talking about a holiday experience you had with an ex, tell him you went with a friend, or a family member instead. The last thing either of you needs at this point is sexual jealousy and him thinking about the last guy you were naked with (not a good image over dinner). Never give him a total of how many lovers you've had – really he shouldn't be asking anyway. If your last man dumped you, then lie about it. He doesn't want to sit there with another man's reject. And it's also entirely acceptable to shave a couple of years off your age if you want to. Don't be afraid to lie about these things. God invented lies for a reason.

Well, those are the general rules.

Any kind of defeatist attitude prior to any date is strictly prohibited!

Play with all the tips I've given you on what to wear, what to say, when to kiss and where to go. But the most important trick of all to learn at this stage is the Scottish shower system.

The Scottish shower technique

'When she was good she was very, very good; but when she was bad she was horrid.'
NURSERY RHYME

Ah, yes. This is the most crucial trick you can learn in these first few pre-sex weeks.
GERRY

Having lived in Scotland for quite a while I can tell you that, as a rule, taking a shower there is a nightmare. The plumbing system is terrible. The water veers between hot and cold constantly.

Girls, you can learn a lot from the Scottish shower system when it comes to men. Blow hot and cold so that he never knows what's coming next. Turn the chemistry on and off by sending slightly mixed signals. Be generally nice to him, but then occasionally aloof and distant to keep him on his toes.

Just when he starts to think he's got you, go cold on him. Keep him guessing. He should never know where you're coming from. One day you're loving and giving and listening to him droning on about his childhood puppy. The next you're completely unattainable.

This technique will baffle him but also feed his addiction to possess and know you. His ego blinds him and he won't be used to what he perceives as an unfair dismissal of his masculine charms. He'll fight harder to get your attention, wonder what on earth the stupid thing was that he did that has put you off him. Men find indifference intoxicating. He'll want further dates because he'll want to figure you out. He'll want to make up for the slight that he has obviously caused. He will be intrigued!

Use my unique, patented Scottish shower technique to make sure you blow hot and cold just enough to keep him on the boil.

The blackjack scoring method
There's an old poker joke: 'Men are

like a deck of cards. You need a heart to love one, a diamond to marry one, a club to smash his head, and a spade to bury the bastard!' Luckily you've got a queen to tell you the rules.

Dating is a lot like playing cards. My unique Scottish shower technique for dating is a bit like playing blackjack.

In blackjack some cards are worth −1 point (all picture cards like jacks and queens, plus the ace). Some are worth +1 point (those between two and seven). The trick in blackjack is to keep count of all your cards and maintain a balance of plus- and minus-scoring cards in your hands worth between 0 and 10. You're in a losing position when your hand is worth over 10 points or a negative number.

It's the same in dating. We have positive and negative actions – let's call them 'blowing hot' and 'blowing cold', like the Scottish shower. Some actions let him think he's in control. Some actions show that you are. The trick is to find a nice balance between the two. Too many nice actions and he'll think you're a doormat or boring. Too many negative actions and he'll think you're too cool, not interested and a bit of a witch.

Here are some examples of positive actions – 'blowing hot' – and negative actions – 'blowing cold' – in the dating game. If you do something nice and warm from the hot list, try and balance it out with a short, chilly blast from the cold list.

Blowing hot actions
- Compliment him on his outfit (even if it's hideous).
- Tell him you love his aftershave and move in close to his neck as you do so.
- Let him order for you in a restaurant. (It'll make him feel knowledgeable and masculine.)
- Laugh at his (extremely bad) jokes.
- Lie and tell him that he has a 'wicked sense of humour'. (For a man this is the next best thing to being told you're good in bed.)
- Be supportive. Don't pile on flattery, but sympathise with and identify with his problems. All men have insecurities and will love this.
- Occasionally overlook his faults. (If you point out his shortcomings he'll just go off and cheat on you because that's his way of seeking revenge.)
- Use your Churchill nodding-dog technique and pretend to listen while he drones on about some tedious business meeting. He'll believe you're really interested, even though your mind is in a retail galaxy far, far away.
- Maintain strong eye contact throughout the date, occasionally staring at his mouth and biting your lips. (Which of course is a subconscious signal to the man that you want him to kiss you.)
- Touch his hand for a second whilst making a point, look him in the eye, then move your hand away.

It drives a man wild and makes him think you're longing to bed him.
- Squeak in 'fear' during a scary movie, so the big strong man can feel all protective by giving you a cuddle.
- Say 'thank you' cutely at the end of the evening and tell him you've had the most wonderful time.

That's all very nice and the man will think you're the best thing ever. But he'll also think that he has you in his pocket, so balance it all out with some cold air, ladies, just to keep him confused.

Blowing cold actions
- During a dinner date, ask him about the food before you order. When he tells you what he thinks you should have, say thank you very much, good idea. Then when the waiter comes, choose the opposite.
- Don't return his text thanking you for 'a wonderful evening' until two days later. And ignore all calls or text messages he sends in between. (I mean it. Send absolutely zilch. This will make him sweat, wondering what he did wrong, what he said that was wrong and if he's *ever* going to get to see you naked.)
- When you do return his calls, don't apologise for the delay. Just say hello.

- When he suggests an evening for another date, say you're busy that day. Make him wait for a day as you check your diary. Then ring during working hours, when you know he'll be too busy to pick up the phone, and leave a lovely – but brief – message telling him when you're free to see him.
- On the early qualifying dates, cut them short, leaving him wishing he'd booked you for longer and wondering where you are going without him.
- When he tries to kiss you (having been driven mad with lust by your flirtatious lip-biting technique), stop him (if you haven't yet had three dates).
- If he tries to put his hands on your hips (before you've been dating three months), you playfully slap them away and tell him 'not tonight'.
- If he buys you a little present (for example, because it is Valentine's Day or Easter, or on a random day because he just thought you were fabulous), say 'thank you' really sweetly. But don't buy him anything back.
- Go on a date with someone else. (There's no need for you to be exclusive in these early stages.)
- If you know he looks through your phone, delete any 'sent' messages that are even vaguely complimentary about him, and delete all his texts in your inbox.
- Keep any Internet dating sites active – and log in occasionally. Just to see what's there.

- Once a month, at least, switch your phone off altogether for a day. Have a nice long bath and don't answer the door. He'll go mad wondering where you are.

Of course, if you're not careful you can end up with a busted flush. The following actions will see you crashing out of the card game of romance no matter how fabulous you are. Think of them as cards worth minus a million points. You're going to have to be very lucky and do an awful lot of clever card work over an awfully long time if you're ever going to counteract these little errors:

Busted flush actions
- Spending a date ranting about how badly exes have treated you. All you're proving to him at this point is that you're not ready for a new man in your life yet.
- Taking phone calls during your date and screeching to your friends, 'I'm with *him* on a *date*!'
- Repeatedly phoning him. You text, get no reply for a day, get panicked and think 'what if he's fallen down a well?' You then call and get the answering machine and leave a message. No reply. You call again, and again … Oh dear. Leave it at one text. If he doesn't reply just move on!
- Talking about erotic exploits with exes. Okay, dear,

he probably guessed you're not a virgin, but there's no need to spell it out.

- Getting legless. Bad girl! If you must drink a lot, then always make sure you're drinking less than him. Slurring your way through the date is not attractive.
- Ordering massively expensive items off the menu, like lobster or the finest champagne, without being invited to. If he suggests it, fine, but you don't want to bankrupt the poor man.
- Having a tantrum or emotional breakdown. Oh, he's going to run a mile, my darling. Tears are completely unacceptable in the early dating stages. He'll see you as high maintenance and exhausting.
- Calling him your 'boyfriend' when it's only date number two.
- Leaving your toothbrush in his bathroom without his permission. (That really represents possessiveness. Carry it in your bag instead!)
- Or, even worse, pointing at diamond rings in jewellery stores as you walk by. My God, woman! What are you playing at? Unforgivable!
- Having sex on a first date. Well, that's minus about three million points. I've said this before. I doubt you'll ever see *him* again, you floozy.

Who should you dump?

Anything on that last little checklist could result in you getting dumped. But of course the decision about whether to go on another date is not entirely up to him.

If the man is not good enough for you, dump him. Don't just be grateful that someone will go on a date with you. Remember, you deserve someone fabulous. You simply haven't got time to date life's losers.

Finding a good partner is like job-hunting. You wouldn't waste your time replying to every single job in the situations vacant pages, would you? You don't have the time to do interviews with every potential employer; you only focus on the jobs that are suited to your abilities, have prospects and will guarantee stability. The same applies to dating. Only date the decent ones. Learn to spot and discard the losers, bores and egomaniacs, not to mention the possible drunks, gamblers, and recreational drug users. Concentrate on the ones who can string a sentence together and seem genuinely interesting and intelligent.

Be selective. This is a choice for life. Even if you actually really like him, even if he is devastatingly handsome, if he isn't right for you, leave him! You cannot fix what my grandmama calls the 'bad eggs'.

Men to avoid like the plague

Men with no drive.

If you're happy to spend your days in romantic poverty, then perhaps this doesn't apply to you. But I think it pays to think about your future and there's no harm in checking their prospects. Ask what car they want, where they want to live, where they went on holiday. If they're students, ask where and what they're studying. Assess and discard the ones that are going nowhere. Drifters may be terribly romantic artistic types who are great to be around, but the romantic artistic act can wear a little thin if you end up working all hours to pay the bills while they sit on the sofa all day, daydreaming about being discovered.

Married men.

A lot of men don't actually mention they're married at first. They hope to reel you in with a few dates before they drop that little bombshell. Or perhaps they just ignore the fact they've got a wife and go on flirting anyway. But do you want to date them? Of course you *can* steal a man from his wife, or long-term partner, but think on ... Have you really got the balls to do this? I know one friend from university who seduced a married man and got him away from his wife. But then the whole department at university knew what she'd done. She was called a man-eater, a home-wrecker; she was whispered about all the time. She couldn't stand the pressure of the gossip and the wrath of the students afterwards. The relationship collapsed.

Girls, I'd say, stay away from married men. I believe that a man with a casual girlfriend is fair play. If he isn't committed to her yet, then there's a chance, and all's fair in love and war. But once she's got a ring on her finger, give up. One, you'll have the pressure of all that gossip. Two, if he cheats on her, he'll probably cheat on you too. And three, his ex may just be an expert with voodoo dolls and cause you a lot of pain for stealing her man.

Boring men.

A man may be rich, he may be handsome, but does he excite you? Ask yourself if you can really stomach waking up next to him for the next twenty years. Imagine growing old and staring at each other in the reflection of the TV set. You need an adventurous man whose spirit doesn't grow old with age. If you have a depressed and boring man it will depress you. If you find someone who has energy for life you will get energy for life.

Stingy men.

What's the point of being with a stingy, miserable guy? If someone's mean on a date, then it's indicative that they will be mean with their feelings as well. Even if the man is not rich, he can put in the effort. Ten pounds will buy a lovely picnic and a walk by a river. If he just sits there saving vouchers for 2-for-1 meal deals and counting the pennies, then you're in for a miserable life, my dears. My darling grandmother and her (second) husband have spent everything they've earned on fur coats, jewellery, rich life experiences, fabulous holidays and a marriage full of memories. That's the way you should live with your man. Grandmama's motto is that even if you've spent all the money, you can always leave your loved ones your diamonds when you go!

Cheaters.

You can spot the type. He'll try and sleep with you after the first date. He'll stare at other females when he's with you. He'll ask you what your opinion is on open relationships. This man is as predictable as Amy Winehouse entering rehab. He – will – cheat. If any man ever cheats on you, dump him. I don't believe in second chances. If he sleeps with somebody else while he is sleeping with you, get rid. I'm a firm believer that once the glass is broken, it cannot be pieced back together. I think it poisons the rest of your life with him. Things will never be the same again. Tell him, wrong pussy, Mr Bond!

The toxic bachelor/narcissist.

This is the type that always texts you with a last minute message saying 'Sorry, Babes, I can't make it.' Babes? How dare he! Unless he has a damn good excuse, then get rid. If not, you'll end up asking yourself the question,

'What's wrong with me?' all the time. The question you should be asking is: 'What's wrong with him?' And the solution is to dump him.

The jealous guy.
If he tries to control you, if he has constant, unfounded suspicions, it will poison your relationship. This man will, bit by bit, curtail and strangle you, your personality and freedom. Jealous men are trouble. Okay, a little bit of male possessiveness is good – it means he's interested in you, and his masculine instincts tell him to protect and preserve his role as your male. But do you really want to live life in a threesome – you, him and his paranoia? Stand up to him from the start. If you get a red warning light over his actions or he mentions his jealous, possessive behaviour with an ex, get rid.

Drinkers.
I don't drink, so I'm sober enough to see what damage it can do to relationships. Does your man binge-drink regularly on a social evening out? Is his drinking out of control? Can he make it through a date without a visit to a pub? I'm not saying you can't date a man who enjoys a pint, but take note if his personality gets distorted though alcohol. Does he become rude and obnoxious to you? Does he do stupid things like trying to drive home? Sharing a bottle of wine together is fine, but do you really want to spend your life looking after a comatose

wreck? If his drinking levels worry you, then leave him. If he ever turns nasty towards you, walk out of the bar immediately and go home alone. And forget him.

Show-offs.
Beware of the ultra extrovert with the constant name-dropping! Work out if he's just nervous and trying to impress you, or a total name-dropping, showing-off bore. People who are obsessed with being seen in the right places with the right people often tend to have personalities like film sets – an impressive façade with a load of flaky plywood behind.

That's the losers sorted. Now, if a man makes it through all these tests, and you still think, after three months, that he's Mr Wonderful, then I have some fabulous news for you.

You can now have sex, you lucky little lady.

PART FOUR

How to Treat Him Mean When You (Finally) Have Sex with Him

'Choose neither a woman nor linen by candlelight.'
ANCIENT PROVERB

Girls, this is the first time he sees his woman and her
bedlinen up close. We're going to use low candlelight
and high cunning.

GERRY

The *mise en place*

I'm hoping that you've waited three months before following the advice in this chapter. (Remember what I said about those *Debrett's* girls.) Our man should be reeled in, emotionally caught up with you and he should have worked hard to get to this point. You should be convinced he's Mr Perfect. He's passed all your tests. He's special.

If you can tick yes to all these, then, my lucky little mammoths, you can *finally* cave in to your caveman. You can have sex with him.

Since you've kept him waiting for so long, let's make it a night to remember. Girls, this is important. Don't take this advice lying down (no pun intended). If you want to ensure a fabulous first-night performance, then preparation is everything.

Back to the *mise en place* theory – we want all the ingredients perfectly in place ready for your big night. The trick here is to prepare massively in advance, yet make it all look spontaneous. You should just automatically appear like a sex goddess.

Underwear

First up, what to wear. Let's start with your knickers. My God I've heard some horror stories from my straight male friends about girls on the first night. One poor man actually took a girl to bed who was wearing knickers and socks marked with the day of the week. She sat there with Monday branded across her bottom. Not a good look. She was dumped before she had a chance to show him Tuesday. Another bought knickers with a built-in condom pocket. Armed and ready – not classy. And then there are those who think it's perfectly fine to turn up in Spanx Pants. What *are* they thinking of? Yes, those great big old granny knickers may make you look amazing with your clothes on, but I'm told they're almost impossible to get off and a vast expanse of straining flesh coloured lycra is not a turn-on.

Down the line there'll be time for him to see you in your big comfortable pants. But get the engagement ring first. Don't let him see the horror knickers in these vital early stages.

If you want help in the waist and stomach department, go for a corset. I know they're not comfortable but they look great, they force you to sit and walk in a sexy manner, and the man will appreciate it.

Oh, and don't wear tights. It's one heck of an anti-climax if you've made him wait three months to undress you and all he finds underneath is a laddered pair of 90 deniers.

Get yourself a really gorgeous set of silk underwear that will make you feel and look amazing. Every woman should have at least one set of fabulous lingerie which is suitable for very special occasions. If you've got the budget, then a trip to Coco de Mer, Agent Provocateur or La Perla is well worth it. Marks & Spencer do cheaper versions which are just as good. Save up, or ask friends to club together to buy you a set for your birthday. It only costs the same as a few rounds of drinks in the pub. If you look after it and hand wash it, it'll last. It's a great investment in your sex life. Plus it'll give the man a few hints too, so when he goes out shopping he goes shopping for lovely silky stuff – not a cheap nylon thong.

Waxing
Body hair. Now, this is a biggie. When I say act like a mammoth, I mean in turns of being chased. I don't want you taking beauty tips from these hairy beasts. Like I've said before, men do moan to me about your body hair, ladies, and I'm afraid that when it comes to first-time sex there are certain things that are a bit of a turn-off for men.

First up, the legs. There are a lot of you out there who just shave from the knee down once a week and hope that'll do, aren't there? Be a bit more thorough, girls. Take a look at yourself in the mirror and ask what needs doing. I've heard tales of hairy tummies, hairy thighs, even hairy nipples. And all could have been sorted out with a tweezer or a visit to a salon with a request for a whole-leg and thorough bikini-line wax and a quick scan through the magnifying glass for any rogue sprouting.

Yes, I know it all hurts, but silky, waxed skin looks and feels amazing. Men will appreciate it as it's so different from our own hairy selves. Take a couple of painkillers beforehand and go for it. Remember, everything should look natural, though. A Brazilian wax is always appreciated by the men I speak to, but don't go asking for his initials to be fashioned into the design in diamanté. If you really can't face the pain of the waxing strip, then do a thorough job with hair removal cream or a razor. Just remember not to leave any shaving cream or Veet out on display in the bathroom. Not sexy. And don't go into details about how much it hurt getting your body hair ripped out. The trick is to pretend all this stuff just happens naturally.

Fake tan

Watch this one. A lot of brands can make you smell like burnt biscuits and leave odd brown streaks all over the sheets and towels. Either have it done a couple of days before, or make sure you've got dark sheets on the bed.

Your body

Hopefully, if you've waited like I told you to, there's been plenty of time to get down the gym so you're looking more fabulous than ever. But don't worry about the odd lump or bump. Trust me, the man is in your bedroom. He's been wanting to sleep with you for three months. He will not be stopped by less than perfect thighs. Besides, curves are good in bed. They make you feel softer. No one wants to sleep with a rock-hard plastic Barbie doll. If a woman has a body which is all muscles and hard perfection, it hints at someone with a bit of a neurotic personality.

Don't worry about cellulite, either. Men have cellulite too, it's just that we've got really hairy legs and bottoms which cover it. (Don't try covering *your* cellulite by growing your leg hair, though – it's not a good look.)

And don't forget that men have insecurities about their own bodies. I've got a round tummy, for example. I think it's disgusting. But men tell me they actually find it cute.

That's your body ready. Now get the house ready.

Hide the evidence

If you're planning the great seduction to be at yours, then have a scout around the house first. Try not to have thousands of bottles of lotions and potions out on display.

He'll visualise you coming into his flat and swamping it. Only have a couple of delicious shower lotions or body creams out on the shelf. Moustache bleaching kits, spot creams or anti-cellulite bottom cream should be banished to the back of a cupboard.

Is there any evidence of exes in the flat? Letters, clothes, photos? Spare toothbrush? Cuddly toys? These things take up emotional space as well as room space. Get rid. You don't want him to think you have men coming round all the time.

Prepare music

Good music is vital to creating the right atmosphere for your big night, but again, you need to make it all feel spontaneous. Look through your record collection and pick tracks that are 'womanly'. Think Nina Simone, Ella Fitzgerald, the big jazz divas. If you've got an iPod you can actually prepare yourself a 'playlist' of seductive music which you casually click on as you walk into the room. If not, have a handy pile of perfect CDs ready. Using the voices of these fabulous women will help seduce your man and you'll also absorb a bit of their mystique.

Avoid male singers though. You want your man to concentrate on the job he's about to take in hand (you). If you suddenly start popping up with Frank Sinatra, Barry White or Dean Martin he might start feeling he can't compete with these great male seducers.

And do watch out for lyrics. Etta James growling 'I

just wanna make love to you' could be quite cute, but singing along to 'It's raining men. Hallelujah!' could spoil things a bit.

Your bedroom

As I've said before, candlelight is an essential bewitching tool as it hides a multitude of faults. It really flatters your features. I use it all the time to con people into thinking I have the perfect figure.

Have candles ready around your home, and particularly, around your bedroom. Pretend that you lounge around by candlelight on a nightly basis. (Keep them away from the curtains and the duvet though, girls – we want the flames of passion, not a real conflagration.)

Make the flat smell nice too. Before you go out for the evening, perhaps pour a few drops of jasmine or patchouli essential oil on an aromatherapy burner or on a piece of fabric placed on a radiator so your house smells gorgeous.

And change your sheets. Okay, I'm as bad as you – I don't always have clean sheets. But I will if I know there's going to be a man in there that night. Have lovely clean sheets that smell of fabric softener and gorgeous things and just happen to be all clean and crisp on your bed.

Oh, and a silk scarf casually draped within reach of the bed is always a winner. Several male friends have recounted *that* little game to me with a smile the morning after. (Not a woolly scarf though! Blindfolding and bondage sessions just don't work with itchy mohair.)

Now, I'm not going to tell you everything. This isn't a sex book, after all. If you need tips, try buying *The Joy of Sex* (although frankly, looking at some of the illustrations, they need to be a bit more thorough in the waxing department).

Don't feel like you have to put on a show, make wild sex talk, swing from the rafters or amaze him with your sexual repertoire. You're not a porn star. Just have fun. Remember, the man is hooked in now, so this will be the first of many times that you make love together. You can act out scenes from *Emmanuelle*, work your way through the *Kama Sutra* or play doctors and nurses for hours in the future.

You've made him wait, he wants you. Trust me, you're going to have a good time tonight. So don't worry. Just put your best knickers on and then enjoy taking them off.

Make love, not coffee

Now a few words of warning, girls. After this first night of passion your brain is going to be flooded with hormones. Let me guess – you're imagining marriage, you're thinking of the perfect children you'll have, and your lifetime of love together.

You can't help all this. It's a chemical reaction. Women react to sex in a different way from men. For women, sex releases oxytocin, the so-called 'cuddle' hormone. You'll turn and look at your man and feel sentimental attachment (even if you secretly thought he was a bit ugly before). You'll be attached. In love. You'll be spending the next day staring at your phone waiting for him to call and propose!

Calm down! It's essential that you remember this is all a chemical reaction in your brain. It's an illusion. A body trick designed to tie you to the man. Sex will increase your heart rate, dilate your pupils, and induce a powerful, all-consuming feeling of euphoria. It's your body's way of making sure you turn to your man and think he's The One. This is all very cute, very addictive and very intoxicating. *But* it also makes you very vulnerable.

The danger at this stage is that you become a lovestruck doormat. Remember – *he's not being flooded with the same hormones*. You know he has fallen for you because he has lusted after you for three months, but this relationship is far from in the bag. You must keep him on his toes. You must continue to play mean!

Think back to the mammoth. The caveman hunter stops running when he captures his prey. Yes, he captured you for one night, but you must make sure you keep him running and let him know the game isn't over yet.

I know you're in a little love bubble, but don't roll over and give your life to him now you're 'intimate.' Of course it's lovely that he can stay the night and cuddle now; your relationship has moved on to a whole new level. But you must still play games. That way he gets to realise that time with you is very important and he has to start thinking about how to ensure that what is happening to him will keep happening.

So put a lid on those feelings and continue to play the game.

Let's start with the morning after. Don't wake up and start cooking him a three-course breakfast to prove your love for him. Instead let him look after you! Smile sweetly. Tell him you want him to make himself feel at home, and he should feel free to help himself in the kitchen. (In other words, can he make you some coffee?)

Think back to the Scottish shower technique. Of course I want you to be lovely and adorable to your man – he is sharing your bed now. But you must keep things in balance to show him you're a fabulous independent woman who still needs to be chased. Play the odd little trick:

✗ Don't return those post-sex texts immediately. Make him wait. Two hours at least. A day is better.

✗ Don't *ever* ask, 'Do you love me?' One friend of mine, Emily, used to think it was 'cute' to tell her new man after only a few dates: 'I think I'm falling in love with you.' It was only meant to show affection, but the men all dumped her, thinking she was (a) needy and (b) two rhubarbs short of a crumble.

✗ Don't be available 24/7. The last thing you want is

for him to take you for granted. Don't be afraid to cherish your friends; always have time for them. Tell your new man 'I have other plans for tonight' and go out with them rather than him. That way he'll understand that your life doesn't revolve around him. I've just made my guinea pig man wait three days before I even called him back to tell him I can't see him. It's good for them.

✗ If you go away on a trip, don't make it blatantly obvious you were pining for him. Just say, 'I was enjoying myself so much I didn't even notice how fast time went. But it's really nice to be back with you.' And never say the forbidden 'I missed you' (unless you're well down the road of the relationship with children and a house and everything).

✗ *Do not* share all your personal troubles. Okay, we all have problems – financial, family or work issues – but if you feel that need to call him and share them all, *put down that phone*! Of course it's tempting, especially if you've been single for some time, but early on, these issues are boring to hear about, and you don't want to come across like that. Call your friends instead and bore them. They know you, they love you – that's what friends are for!

✗ Don't talk about your exes. (I'll say this again and again, until it's imprinted on your tiny grey cells!) Okay, he knows you're not a virgin, but there's no need to give him details.

✗ Don't talk about his exes either. When you're in his bed, he should be thinking only about you.

✗ Don't introduce him to all your friends too soon. He might feel like a trophy, 'shown off' by you to your entourage. I'd say two months of serious dating should be enough.

✗ Don't ignore him when you go out with the girls. Men have moaned to me about women that go off in pairs and gossip together like Statler and Waldorf, the two old men in the balcony of *The Muppet Show*. Save your gossiping for your girls only nights out.

✗ Don't share the details of any shopping trips. You may love to admire your Gucci bag and Swarovski-encrusted mobiles. But he will be petrified about his future American Express bills.

✗ If Valentine's Day crops up around this time in the early stages of a relationship, don't send him a card or give him a present. Of course, he should send *you* flowers and little missives, but unless the relationship is very well established, sending gifts looks possessive.

✗ Don't start talking about 'us' all the time to your friends, or buying joint presents for friends.

✗ Don't start discussing children's names.

✗ Don't leave items at his house, like a toothbrush or clothes, unless invited to do so.

✓ Do play some games to make him jealous. A card on Valentine's Day sent from you to you is not a bad way to make him a bit jealous and ring some alarm bells. Say you've no idea who sent it – you thought it was him!

✓ And, I've said it before – *switch off that phone*. Disappear for a day. Keep him on his toes and make him wonder where you are. And who you're with. Even if all you were doing was watching *Sex and the City* on your own.

Treating the man mean is not the only trick you have to learn at this stage. You have to cope with his friends and family too.

His friends and family

His best friends

Beware of some of his best friends, especially if they're not happy with their love life.

Of course, I may be misjudging them all. They may be super friends who are delighted for him that he has found someone. But in the vast majority of cases, I'd say stay on your toes.

The problem with single mates is that they want your man to themselves. Single men don't want their male mates to have a girlfriend. They want him to sit around with them, playing their Xbox and moaning about women. And single women don't want their single male friends to couple up either, because they want him to escort them on nights out.

Don't underestimate these people: the influence they have over him is immense and powerful. They can nip your romance in the bud easily. All it takes is for a game of football with the lads, and one of them to drop a casual, 'She's not my type but I'm glad you're happy' (translation: 'You can do so much better, dude'), and it's over.

One good trick with these people is always to pretend that you like them. Avoid criticising them at all costs. Tell your man that you find his male friends witty and fabulous. Even if his female friends are being complete cows, never, *ever* slag them off. Do the reverse. Praise them. (Go on, grit your teeth and do it!)

This has two advantages. One, he will pass the message on, and if they've been slagging you off they'll feel guilty and start being nicer to you. And two, if they all turn round and start slagging you off to him, he'll think, 'Oh, what a bunch of gits. And my girlfriend was really nice about them.'

Just go home and bitch about them all to your mates instead.

His mother

There's a school of thought that men are sometimes subconsciously looking for a younger version of their mother, but don't try and become a clone of her. You really don't want him to think of you in the same way he thinks of a woman who is thirty years older than you and used to change his nappies, do you?

As with his friends, never, ever slag off his mother, or anyone in his family, come to that. (To his face, I mean – say what you like to your friends behind his back.) And if he starts criticising his family himself, nod sympathetically but don't join in. Remember that whatever you say will get back to them one day. The last thing you need is a mother-in-law from hell.

The ex
Will that bitch just not go away? This is a tricky one. If they share children, then I'm sorry, but you're just going to have to put up with her. But if she's just lingering around like a bad smell out of habit, then you'll have to play mean to get rid of her.

First up, never, ever show any signs of jealousy, annoyance or a possessive nature when it comes to his ex. Even if you hate her. Remember that she is the ex. They have ended it. You are the current. Don't feel insecure or think that you have to compete. She's probably jealous of you, because you're the one under the duvet with him each night.

Be lovely to her, and tell yourself that eventually the sad little witch will go away and get her own life and her own boyfriend.

Meanwhile, start to ask him, subtly and casually, why they split up. Make him dredge up all those bad memories of their fights. Then nod a lot, look really sympathetic and look shocked when he tells you her faults. Say 'Oh my God!' a lot in an astounded voice and agree with him whole-heartedly about his (no doubt heavily skewed) version of events. He'll be subconsciously thinking how unlike her you are, and how lucky he is to have survived his time with the psycho bitch ex from hell and found fabulous you instead.

Of course, to him, you're coming across as the understanding other half with whom he can share his problems. The reality is that you're making him re-evaluate all the time he spends with his ex. You're making him realise that she's not a trusted friend with a shared past as a lover that he should talk to and confide in. She's a cow who terrorised his life for years.

Drop hints about how lucky you are that you no longer have to be in constant touch with your ex. That you've been strong and moved on. Say things like, 'Once the crystal has broken it can never be glued back together.' This will make him aspire to be like you. Make him consider that being in touch with his ex is actually a sign of weakness.

All this sounds really devious. But then, she's being a devious little cow by hanging round your man and bitching about you, isn't she?

Is he going to propose?

*'My mother says I didn't open my eyes for eight days after
I was born, but when I did, the first thing I saw was
an engagement ring. I was hooked.'*
ELIZABETH TAYLOR

I can't quite promise you the Taylor-Burton,
but if you desire those diamonds, let's get you some.

GERRY

Okay. You've found your Mr Perfect. You're dating and you're happy. For some of you this is where I leave you – happily loved-up in dating bliss. Staying with Mr Perfect. (Until you get bored of him and move on to another Mr Perfect.) Congratulations, and don't forget to email me and tell me so I know that the weight gain and sad reading shelf have been worth it.

But some girls tell me they want that rock on their finger. In case that's you, let's give you some tips on how to get him down the aisle.

First of all, let's make sure you're 'exclusive'. Of course, if you waited three months like I told you, he will have been committed to you and your relationship by the time you came to bed him.

If you didn't quite make this deadline and you're not quite sure you're the only girl in his bed, say something like, 'If someone else asked you out on a date, would you go?'

If he says 'Yes' or 'Depends', I'd move on. He's a player. Hopefully, if you've played by all my mean rules he will reply 'No', at which you smile and reply, 'Neither would I. I'm very pleased with what I've got.'

So you're exclusive. That's a good sign. Now, if you're after wandering down the aisle in a white frock, what do you do next?

First of all you must continue to use all the tips that I've outlined in the previous chapters. Sometimes the man will propose within a matter of months, but on average I'd say it takes about two years.

Here are some good signs that he may well ask you to marry him:

- ✓ You've met all of his friends and family, and you're known to all of them as a couple. If he goes to visit his parents on his own all the time and you've never met them, then I'm afraid he probably doesn't view you as The One.
- ✓ His friends are married. If he acted as best man at any of their weddings, this is an excellent sign. If his mates are all single guys, this is a bad sign. They won't want to encourage him to settle down. A good technique that a friend of mine tried was to encourage her man to spend some great evenings with her happily married friends. This helped balance the negative influence of his single friends.
- ✓ If he was married before, he has now got over his

divorce and he doesn't still moan on about his nightmare first wife.

✓ He reads the travel pages in the weekend papers avidly and drops hints about dream honeymoon destinations.

All these are good signs, but if you're still waiting for that rock after two years you need to take a bit more action. A good trick is to drop key phrases into conversation. Things like, 'We make such a good team don't we, you and I?' or, 'We work well together.' That should give him the hint that he'd better hang on to you for life.

If you're still getting nowhere, then sometimes you may have to play dirty. If he's never mentioned anything like buying a house together, or says things like, 'We can't afford to get married,' or seems to be still living the life of a single guy, then you may have to start playing games.

One technique used by Greek girls all the time is to make him jealous. Create a love triangle with another man who's fighting for your attention. Don't worry about finding another suitor – just make one up. Start to drop his name in conversation. His name could be Graham or Nick; he could be an Italian named Paolo or a tall, blond Scandinavian Viking called Olaf! You can give him whatever attributes you want. If your boyfriend wants to be a senior businessman, say your man is the director of a company. If your man is short, say his rival is tall. Worried about his weight? His rival runs marathons. Say you met him through work. Say things like, 'Oh, he sends me emails and I really can't just get rid of him.' That should put the cat among the pigeons.

Of course, I'm only recommending that you have a mythical man. Don't cheat on him with a real one. Remember Helen of Troy? She left her husband to run off with Paris (or Orlando Bloom, if you watched the movie), but that caused the Trojan war *and* her husband almost stabbed her before he took her back. Best to keep the other man as a figment of your imagination, girls.

Okay, this love rival is merely a ghost, but I'm all for jealousy. It really works. It's good to make the man a little bit possessive. Yes, it's devious, but the ends justify the means. It's his fault, because he should have proposed.

Another trick is to keep disappearing. Go away with the girls on holiday instead of going with him. Become busier at work. That sort of thing. That way he'll want to see more of you, and start to realise that unless he proposes, there is no guarantee he can see you.

A final ultimatum is to disappear altogether. Ask him how he feels about you together. If he says he isn't sure whether he wants to commit, or makes some excuse up, then disappear. If you're living together, move out. Harsh, I know, and he may not chase you. That's the problem with ultimatums – you don't always get the response you want. But if it's marriage that you're after it's the best chance you have of making him decide.

As he sits alone, he may just realise that he needs you. But if he doesn't, then he probably never was your Mr Perfect. Don't waste any time. Remember *you* treat *men* mean, not the other way round. Move on. Go back to Part One and start again.

You're hitched!

If he does propose, congratulations! But girls, you still need to keep him on his toes. Take a tip from our little Greek *ponires*. There's a part of the Greek Orthodox wedding ceremony where the priest tells the bride and groom: 'The woman should fear the man.' At this point it is traditional for the woman to stamp on the man's foot. Just to show him she's boss.

Remember, the woman is always in control. She treats him mean all the way up to the altar. He should be grateful when you tell him 'I do.'

Married life

And don't assume that a ring on your finger means you should stop playing games, either. Always treat your man mean. Always be in control. As they say in *My Big Fat Greek Wedding*, men always think they're the head of the household. But the woman is the neck, so it's up to her which direction the head turns in.

Wear make-up, look fantastic, seduce him with body language and words and actions. Don't get blind drunk in front of him. Don't cry. Don't wail. Don't sob that you love him and be a doormat. Treat him mean until you're both very, very old. Follow the Scottish shower technique every day, even when you're so old that your great-great-grandchildren are visiting. Keep him on his toes even if he uses a Zimmer frame. It's good for him.

In fact, ideally, the only day when you can drop the mean act, give him a break and confess that you've loved him all along, tell him he's perfect, you're lucky to have him and you got all this advice out of this book, is the day when you're absolutely certain that he's on his deathbed.

EPILOGUE

'A wealthy Athenian was making a sea voyage with some companions. A terrible storm blew up and the ship capsized. All the other passengers started to swim, but the Athenian kept praying to the goddess Athena, making all kinds of promises if only she would save him. Then one of the other shipwrecked passengers swam past him and said, "While you pray to Athena, start moving your arms!"'

THE SHIPWRECKED MAN AND ATHENA,
AESOP'S FABLES

Girls, I can only help so far. Now you must act!
Get paddling. And get a man.

GERRY

My dear single friends, I've given you the ammunition, but now you have to act on it. Revolutionise your life! Get your man!

Yes, I know, I've gone all Lenin on you again. But I mean it! Keep being determined, keep being relentless and keep looking.

These tips work. But you must *use* them, not just read them. Stop being so nice to your men. We don't like it. It doesn't work for us.

Remember, you're a catch. Make us work to catch you.

Keep treating him mean. Keep your own life. Keep him guessing. This is the way to tame him, and only then he will belong to you.

Other women may tell you this stuff doesn't work. They may tell you that if you follow these techniques you'll be seen as arrogant, cold, ruthless, controlling. You'll be seen as someone who wastes time playing games.

Don't listen. Let them carry on being nice. And carry on being single. So what if they think you're a bitch? When you get your man, I guarantee they'll be thinking you're a *lucky* bitch.

You've got the information. Now get out there and enjoy it. Go get that man!

Warning !
Keep this book away from your men!

Acknowledgements

I want to thank:

First of all, all the girls who took their time to share strategies, trade secrets and impart a little of their female wisdom to me, and all the men who told me what they loathe, what makes them tick and what electrifies them in a woman. Their stories inspired me and influenced the direction of this dating action plan;

Mum Eufimia, my grandmamas Martha and Anastasia and my great-grandma Maria Vallerio, all extraordinary women, who nourished me and have provided unconditional love throughout my life;

Tom Dawnay for his invaluable insights and generous advice and anecdotes. Eugenia Vrettos, without whose guidance this book wouldn't have been written. My gorgeous editor Sharon Marshall, and charming publisher Rosemary Davidson, who believed in this project and exhibited Olympian patience with my delayed drafts;

My agents Paul Scates and Kevin Newton, Louise Rhind-Tutt, Jenny Rowley and Judith Skorupski my magnificent publicists, Kay Peddle at Random House, and my lawyer, Takis Tsirikos, for protecting me from marauding sharks.

A huge thank you to Silvia Pana, Elena Mastromauro, her mum Urania, Christian Albu and Arnaki for their endless support; also to beloved Lou Lou for chaperoning me in those frenzied days after my eviction from the *BB* asylum; and to everyone else who was there for me and offered feedback for this book, especially Antonis, Amjad, Andrew, Ben, Constantina, Niko, Christina, Mariana, Magda, Tolis, Katerina, Irene, Marina, Mixalis, Sorina, Duncan, Cathy, Craig, Christopher, Marshall, Nat, Paolo, Dan, Dick and Dolly, Suzie, little sister Marsia, my darling twinnies Sam and Amanda, Dee and Dermot, Chanelle, Alison Freeman, Lizzie Cundy, Paul Crompton, Phil Edgar-Jones, Jimmy, Anna-Maria, and Freddy the monkey.

Please send me your feedback

Did I overlook something? Have you developed your own successful techniques, catchphrases or dating strategies you would like to share? Is there something from my advice that hasn't worked? Please send me your feedback on *Gerryster@yahoo.co.uk*

FURTHER READING

I spent most of last year reading dating books to
bring you this advice ...

Some of the best

Argov, S. *Why Men Love Bitches*. Adams Media, Avon Massachusetts, 2004.

Sherry Argov has the most terrible hair. She wears it down
to her feet. Maybe on cold winter days she uses it as a blanket.
But she does give good advice. She must be a little bit of a
bitch herself, I think, but her tips are amongst the best in the
business. She's also very good at explaining how women all
start changing to try to please their man. If she can get a man
with that haircut using this advice, then it's worth following.
She also later wrote *Why Men Marry Bitches*, which is worth
a read, too.

Fein, E., and Schneider, S. *The Rules*. Thorsons, London,
1995.

The Rules series are classic reading on dating – they're the
Jane Eyre of dating books. A lot of the Rules work, but for

me the problem is that they're so very rigid about everything. It's very formulaic, and you can turn into a bit of a robot if you follow them word for word. Another issue is that it's sold so many copies that men can spot the techniques a mile off. I've actually had men come up to me and say: 'Oh God, I had this date, and she so was playing by *The Rules*.' It's also very American – and European men sometimes need a bit more encouragement to ask women on a date. So read, but don't necessarily follow.

Gray, J. *Men Are from Mars, Women Are from Venus*. Thorsons, London, 1993.

This book is a little outdated now. It's also aimed at the American market, so not all of it is relevant for British women, but it's still a classic read and has sold millions of copies. This book will teach you to start noticing patterns in male behaviour and how to understand what they're thinking. But we're not from different planets really. Men and women have a lot in common. Men are from Earth and they want love. Just like you.

Greene, R. *The Art of Seduction*, Profile Books, London, 2001.

This is a treasure trove of seducers from history. It reads like a series of mini biographical novels put together and teaches you seduction from a historical perspective. Okay, we can't all start acting like Cleopatra or Don Juan in the modern-day office environment, but this book gives an interesting interpretation of their lives and techniques. History teaches us. Maybe the seducers from the past will show you a trick or two that helps you entrance a lover in the future.

Gorman-Newman, R. *How to Marry a Mensch*, Fair Winds Press, Gloucester, Massachusetts, 2007.

Even if you're not Jewish, it's worth reading this for tips. Jewish women are wise and aspirational with accumulated centuries of wisdom behind them, and, as Joan Rivers would say, they know how to get the best rings. There are some good lessons to be learned on life in here.

Lowndes, L. *Updating: How to Date Out of Your League*, McGraw-Hill, New York, 2004.

This American author used to be a Pan Am flight attendant. Back then, in the Dark Ages, it was a very glamorous profession. She's good but dare I say it, she comes across as a bit of a golddigger. I don't agree with everything she writes, but I do agree that women should go for quality men, and she will teach you how to get them. She is a wise, matronly type who gives some wonderful tips even though they're a bit extreme. For example, she advises moving to a good area to make sure you meet the right man, even if all you can afford is a shoebox there. Not a bad tip. But if all you can afford is a basement flat, do bear in mind that the lack of sunlight will be terrible for your complexion.

Nakamoto, S. *Men are like Fish*, Java Books, Huntington Beach, California, 2006.

Try this gentleman, Steve Nakamoto. He writes some great lists of advice which are easy to follow, for example why a man didn't call back (never let him see an old photograph of you in which you were unattractive) or 101 places to go to find men (have you considered attending a Fear of Flying seminar?) The back-cover pic of him with a rose is very cheesy, though – how did he ever pull with that?

Papadopoulos, L. *The Man Manual*, Hodder and Stoughton, London, 2005.

I have to put this one in because it's a great book and dearest Linda Papadopoulos is Greek and she's a darling. I will always support the Greeks. We have a saying in Greece – if you don't support your own house, it will fall on you. Without the likes of Linda Papadopoulos, Nana Mouskouri, Telly Savalas and George Michael, we'd be nothing.

Pease, A. and Pease, B. *The Definitive Book of Body Language*, Orion, London, 2006.

A million-selling classic based on a series of psychological journals. It takes a massive area of psychology and popularises it, outlining it step by step. What people say is often very different from what they think or feel: it helps you to read other people's thoughts by their gestures. It's very good if you want some tips on flirting. It also takes a really interesting look at historical figures.

The rest of the shelf

These are the contents of that sad bookshelf I told you about:

Artsrunik, V. *How to Flirt and Be Seductive*, Artnic Media, London, 2003.

Balfour, M. *Smart Dating: How to Find Your Man*, Element, London, 2004.

Behrendt, G., and Ruotola, A. *It's Called a Break-up Because It's Broken*, Harper Element, London, 2005.

Brooks, Y., and Cray, C. *Humped Me, Dumped Me.* Michael O'Mara Books, London, 2005

Browne, J. *Dating for Dummies*. Wiley Publishing, Indiana, 2006

Carmichael, N. *Dating: The Virgin Guide*. Virgin Books, London, 2003.

Carter, S., and Sokol, J. *Men Like Women Who Like Themselves (and Other Secrets that the Smartest Women Know)*. Dell Publishing, New York, 1996.

Carter, S. and Sokol, J. *What Smart Women Know*. M. Evans and Co., New York, 1999.

Copeland, D. and Louis, R. *How to Succeed with Men*. Prentice Hall, New York, 2000.

Cox, T. *Superdate: How to Be One, How to Get One*. Dorling Kindersley, London, 2005.

De Angelis, B. *Secrets About Men Every Woman Should Know*. Thorsons, New York, 1998.

Della Casa, B. *Cinderella Was a Liar: The Real Reason You Can Find a Prince*. McGraw-Hill, Berkshire USA, 2007.

Epstein, N., and Moore, D. L. *The Technique of the Love Affair*. Castle Books, New Jersey, 2002.

Erickson, J. *How to Influence People and Get What You Want*. Hodder and Stoughton, London, 2004.

Greenwald, R. *The Program: Fifteen Steps to Finding a Husband After Thirty*. Time Warner, London, 2004.

Helmanis, L. *Master Dating: Get the Life and Love You Want*. Infinite Ideas, Oxford, 2005.

Hemmings, J. *The Dating Game*. New Holland Publishers, London, 2003.

Hill, H. *Baby Its You: What You Can Do to Find True Love*. Emmis Books, Cincinnati, 2004.

Ivens, S. *A Modern Girl's Guide to Dynamic Dating*. Piatkus Books, London, 2003.

Jillson, J. *The Fine Art of Flirting*. Simon and Schuster,

London, 1986.

Kerner, I. *Be Honest: You're Not That into Him Either*. Harper Collins, New York, 2005.

Kerner, I. *Dsi: Date Scene Investigation: The Diagnostic Manual of Dating Disorders*. Harper Collins, New York, 2006.

Langford, L. *If It's Love You Want, Why Settle for Just Sex?* Prima Publishing, California, 1997.

Marc-Katz, E. and Holmes, L. *Why Are You Still Single*. Penguin, London, 2006.

McGraw, P. *Love Smart: Find the One You Want, Fix the One You Got*. Simon & Schuster, London, 2006.

McKnight, T. W., and Phillips, R. H. *Love Tactics: How to Win The One You Want*. Square One Publishers, New York, 2002.

Miller, R. *Man Magnet: How to Be the Best Woman You Can Be in Order to Get the Best Man*. The Book Factory, London, 2005.

Norwood, M. *Sex and the Married Girl*. Hodder & Stoughton, London, 2005.

Page, S. *If I'm So Wonderful, Why Am I Still Single?* Piatkus Books, London, 2006.

Pease, A. and Pease, B. *Why Men Don't Listen and Women Can't Read Maps*. Orion, London, 2001.

Rabin, S. *How to Attract Anyone, Anytime, Anyplace*. Penguin, London, 1993.

Slotnick, N. *Turn Your Cablight On*. Gotham Books, New York, 2006.

Staples, C. *Everything I Know About Men I Learned from My Dog*. Crombie Jardine Publishing, New York, 2005.

Sullivan, C. J. *Dating Up, Dump the Schlump and Find a Quality Man*. Warner, New York, 2007.

Taylor, K. *Not Tonight, Mr Right*. Penguin, London, 2007.

Worick, J. *The Dating Game*. Collins & Brown, London, 2003.

Wortzel, E. *Bitch*, Quartet Books, London, 1998

Wortzel, E. *The Bitch Rules*. Quartet Books, London, 2001.

Zaric, D., and Kosmas, J. *You Didn't Hear It From Us*. Element, London, 2006

Zinczenko, D. *What Women Don't Know about Men, Love and Sex, Could Fill a Book*. Rodale International Ltd, London, 2007.